THE SHOOTING SCRIPT™

THE ICE STORM

THE ICE STORM

SCREENPLAY, INTRODUCTION, AND NOTES BY
JAMES SCHAMUS

BASED ON THE NOVEL BY RICK MOODY

PREFACE BY
ANG LEE

NHB Shooting Scripts
NICK HERN BOOKS • LONDON

This book first published in Great Britain in 1997 as an original
paperback by Nick Hern Books Ltd., 14 Larden Road, London W3 7ST,
by arrangement with Newmarket Press, New York.

A CIP catalogue record of this book is available from the British Library.

ISBN 1-85459-322-6

Book design by Tania Garcia.
Manufactured in the United States of America.

THE NHB SHOOTING SCRIPT SERIES

The Age of Innocence
I Went Down
The Ice Storm
Jude
The People vs. Larry Flynt
The Shawshank Redemption

For information on forthcoming titles, please contact the publishers:
NHB, 14 Larden Road, London, W3 7ST
e-mail: info@nickhernbooks.demon.co.uk

CONTENTS

For their help with the preparation of this volume, the author would like to thank Jeff Knapp, Nancy Kricorian, Kelly Miller, and Nevette Previd.

PREFACE

BY ANG LEE

When I think of *The Ice Storm,* I think first of water and rain, of how it falls everywhere, seeps into everything, forms underground rivers, and helps to shape a landscape. And also, when calm, of how it forms a reflective surface, like glass, in which the world reappears. Then, as the temperature drops, what was only water freezes. Its structure can crush concrete and push iron away, it is so strong. Its pattern overthrows everything.

This is the structure I have hoped to create in my movie, *The Ice Storm.* Whatever the surface patterns you might see reflected there, the customs and morals, and hopes, and loves of the characters are infused, and overturned, and reestablished by the force of nature that the storm represents.

When I read Rick Moody's novel, I knew immediately that I wanted to make it into a film. For me, such a revelation comes through small details and particular moments. In this case, it was the moment at the end of the novel when Paul is joined at the train station by his family. The power of the novel is to make of this moment no more and no less than what it is. It is an image that has the force of memory, and for that reason an image that has more meaning than any theme or story or even emotion can give it.

I also thought a great deal about the sounds that an ice storm would make, not just the howling of the wind and rain, but the sounds that come afterwards, as the entire world becomes covered in transparent crackling glass. It was these elemental feelings that brought me to *The Ice Storm.* From there, through the pre-production process, I began to see how important the social and historical side of the book was, and how Rick Moody, through the individual stories he told, was exploring the greatest themes of American history and experience. My producers and I often joked that 1973 was America's most "embarrassing" year, with Nixon, polyester, the admitting of defeat in Vietnam, stagflation, the energy crisis. But embarrassment can be a profound and enlightening experience. In researching for the film, my production team and I read many of the novels and self-help books from the period, and watched many movies made in the early seventies. Rather than approach the period as one of "kitsch," this process led us to a tremendous respect and humility. It turned out that there were many truths buried inside the pop psychology and sometimes painfully naive self-help philosophies of the day, and that we two decades later have much to learn from this "embarrassing" past.

INTRODUCTION

BY JAMES SCHAMUS

CENSORING *THE ICE STORM*

Rick Moody's 1994 novel *The Ice Storm* plays a neat trick, and a decid-edly uncinematic one. Told in a knowing, omniscient voice, the book reveals in its final page that that voice is in fact owned by one of the ensemble of the novel's characters. That revelation is a moment of great power, for it is a turn that makes of the novel's story an act of remembering, a search for meaning and truth by someone who, in the most fundamental way, *survived.* Moody has until that final moment played brilliantly on the literary and emotional tension that comes from the contrast between the third-person telling of the story and the particular character of the voice of that telling. It's an old and fruitful tension: To the extent a narrator has a charac-ter, a voice, a personality, how could that narrator be omniscient, all-knowing? Wouldn't he or she be a simple, limited mortal like the rest of us?

To write, especially from memory, and especially into fiction, is to take our first-person limitations and test them against the rigors of a third-person imagination. Such an endeavor may be mere hubristic folly, but it is often just this folly that enables us to widen the scope of our recognitions.

Narrative film, in most of its current incarnations, has a hard time engag-ing in this fruitful tension. Our storytelling conventions, especially in Hollywood, make the cinema an emphatically third-person activity, as if the simple mechanics of film technology cowed us into shying away from more first-person approaches. Hollywood has from time to time toyed with first-person narration, as in Robert Montgomery's *Lady in the Lake,* where a combination of voice-over and continuous point-of-view shots attempted the job. But there's usually something tiresome about the effects, and such experiments have succeeded mainly in the great avant-garde personal cinemas (and videos—another topic) of filmmakers like Chris Marker, Michael Wallin, Jonas Mekas, and Su Friedrich.

So in adapting the novel for the screen, we were faced with an immediate technical problem: Could we find some kind of filmic equivalent to the novel's powerful literary devices, one that retained at least some hint of the book's emotional and philosophical grandeur? The answer, unsurprisingly, was no.

Instead, we came up with a series of *ad hoc* approaches that we hope, in total, might do the trick. While the novel unfolds during a single twenty-four-hour period, filling in its back story through running commentary, we created an entire first hour of the film from hints dropped by Moody in that commentary, picking up where the novel begins about halfway through the script. We turned voice into action.

More important, the novel frequently allows its characters to act in hilariously ill-advised ways while still retaining the reader's sympathies. But reading, for example, about Paul's horrifically endearing bout of masturbation at Libbets's apartment is one thing—seeing it would have been something else altogether, in particular if that image were stripped of the help the book's narrator gives us in appreciating the moment in all its pathos and humor. Without the defining echo of the book's implied first person, the scene (and many others like it) would read as pruriently desperate, especially if thrown explicitly against the screen.

So we found ourselves censoring—censoring not so much the images and scenes from the book but the very voice that had originally made sense of them. It is in such acts of silencing that, I suppose, most adaptations define themselves. I can only hope that the final result is itself a compelling enough testament to the respect and admiration that started the whole process off in the first place.

MAKING *THE ICE STORM*

The shooting script published here is the draft we went into pre-production with. The finished film is quite a different animal. Freak snow storms, equipment failures, sick actors, lack of time, and the hundreds of other contingencies that make up a film shoot all intervened to cause the usual assortment of changes. Some of the scenes you'll read were never shot (the therapy scenes—an homage to late sixties' and seventies' films like Paul Mazursky's wonderful *Bob & Carol & Ted & Alice*—were cut simply because we ran over-time and decided they were expendable); other scenes got left on the editing room floor, mainly because Ang's first cut of the film was over two and a half hours long and something had to go. A shooting script, at the end of the day, is simply a series of suggestions to the director, cast, and crew about how to use their time and spend the film's budget. The more coherent those suggestions, the better. Best of all is when they serve merely as a pretext and foundation for the collective experience of surprise and discovery that makes filmmaking so much fun—and films so different from their scripts.

Shooting commenced on a chilly morning in April 1996, in Waveny Park, New Canaan. As is now usual with Ang Lee's films, the day began with a "Big Luck" ceremony, at which crew, cast, and friends all gather and bow, incense in hand, to the four corners of the earth. Ang stands before the group, and, after a moment's silence and the final bow, he bangs a gong and invites the crowd to share some of the ceremonial feast laid out on a table before them. It's a ceremony both mildly ridiculous and surprisingly effective in its communal impact. On *The Wedding Banquet,* the young nonunion crew crowded the sidewalk across the street from New York's City Hall on a busy Monday morning, as politicians and bureaucrats pushed by us; on *Sense and Sensibility,* the grizzled English crew stood before the imposing Saltram House manor in Devon, joined by Emma Thompson and Kate Winslet in their silk Empire dresses and hair curlers. *The Ice Storm* assembly, with our cast in their garish seventies' outfits, was witnessed by a few of New Canaan's wealthy denizens and their dogs who happened to be passing by on their morning walks.

Whatever Big Luck the ceremony brought was not in the weather department. By midday the sky had turned from gray to icy white, and soon after our first shot, of Kevin Kline walking through the woods, the snow began to fall. As everyone who worked on the film soon learned, snow storms and ice storms are two very different things—ice storms are in fact rain storms during which the temperature falls below freezing—but we decided to keep shooting anyway, and you can see the snow falling as Kevin Kline lifts Christina Ricci on their walk home from the Carvers'. (We shot a swiftly written newscast explaining the day's "light snowfall turning to heavy rains" later on in the shoot.)

As we settled into New Canaan for our first month of shooting, it quickly became apparent that many of the local townspeople were not overjoyed by our presence. The reasons were both specific and general. On the general side, one supposes that the reason people spend as much as they do to live in wealthy hamlets like New Canaan is precisely so they can avoid things like film crews in their midst. Traffic disruptions, crowds of onlookers, and blocks of parked trucks, trailers, and minivans didn't blend easily with the quaint storefronts and Colonial-style mansions. As for specifics, many of the townspeople had read Rick Moody's novel, and a few of them made vocal and very public note of its frank depiction of the sexual revolution's impact on the community circa 1973. Rick had grown up in New Canaan, so there was a particular *roman à clef* intensity to the gossip surrounding the book's contents. The result was a stampede of sales of the book at local bookstores and scores of recalls of the copies remaining in the public library.

As one could imagine, initial local press was at first suspicious. But, thankfully, as the weeks unfolded, the tide turned, and the community began to accept our temporary presence. A copy of the script was deposited on reserve at the library for anyone interested in reading it, and a host of letters to the editor of the *Advertizer* came to the defense of our mores and our shooting habits. Hundreds of people turned out on the weekends during the unseasonably hot spring days as we shot the closing scene of the film at the New Canaan train station, where they witnessed our art department transforming the center of town into a sparkling winter wonderland under the eighty-five-degree heat of the blazing sun.

With the weather alternating between heat waves and torrential downpours, the first half of the shoot was transformed into a frantic race against the first appearance of the leaves and buds of May. Since the action of the film supposedly takes place during Thanksgiving, we were constantly tilting the camera away from the riotous bursts of forsythia that seemed to be constantly dogging us. Careful observers of the film will find the odd patch of deciduous green, but overall Ang and cinematographer Fred Elmes, with the help of a dedicated greens department, were able to keep the color tones of the film limited to a muted, fall-like palette.

The final days of the film were spent at the Harlem Armory in New York, where, in the cavernous expanse of its city-block-wide hall, vaulted by a tin roof, we built the Halford key party set and the Carver house basement. Sharing late night meals of fried chicken and collard greens from Sylvia's Restaurant while taking a break from the "Nixon mask" scene could hardly have underscored more the disjunctions between the happy realities of film production and the illusions eventually projected on the film screen.

Over time, film crews become something like extended families, and on *Ice Storm* there were the usual pranks (anyone caught dozing on set was mercilessly Polaroided, usually after the prop department had placed a few beer and vodka bottles around the unsuspecting sleeper). But even more, there was a sense of connection to many of the specific scenes and events in the film. When developing the script, Ang would often ask about the realism of various parts of the action, such as the shoplifting scenes: Would a privileged American girl really do that? Our answer: Ask just about any woman on the crew when we get there. The bong in Paul's dorm room elicited more than a few knowing nods from many of our straightlaced, settled-down family men on set as did the reel-to-reel tape players and bean bag chairs.

But it wasn't *nostalgia* people were feeling. More often than not, a simple sighting of Elijah Wood's and Adam Hann-Byrd's two-tone bell bottoms would sober up even the most rose-tinted observer. The seventies, except for the people *born* during them (many of whom appear actually to be *enthused* by polyester in the current fashion season), tend not to elicit much allegiance from the people who lived through them. Rather, there's a wistful and communally shared sense of relief at having made it safely past the era and, for many people, a sense of genuine surprise that, in fact, many of the songs, books, fashions, and movies of the period are actually *worth* remembering.

Being on a film crew means being surrounded, day in and day out, with the artifacts of the culture and time you are depicting, and there's something about that physical proximity to the material culture of another world that can be very unnerving. As we continued to live in and explore the world of the seventies we were so painstakingly re-creating, we would again and again witness fellow crew members whose first instinct on encountering some long-forgotten shred of cultural detritus (a song, a car, a Marimekko curtain) was to recoil and then, after a thoughtful pause, to reflect and to remember. The Carver rec room seemed, in particular, to provide a mildly therapeutic space, a kind of architectural encounter room, where those who had passed their adolescences in seventies-style angst could receive a few hurried moments of posttraumatic recollection between camera setups.

I always hope that some of that sense of collective energy can be passed directly from the crew onto the screen, and that the script doesn't get too much in the way.

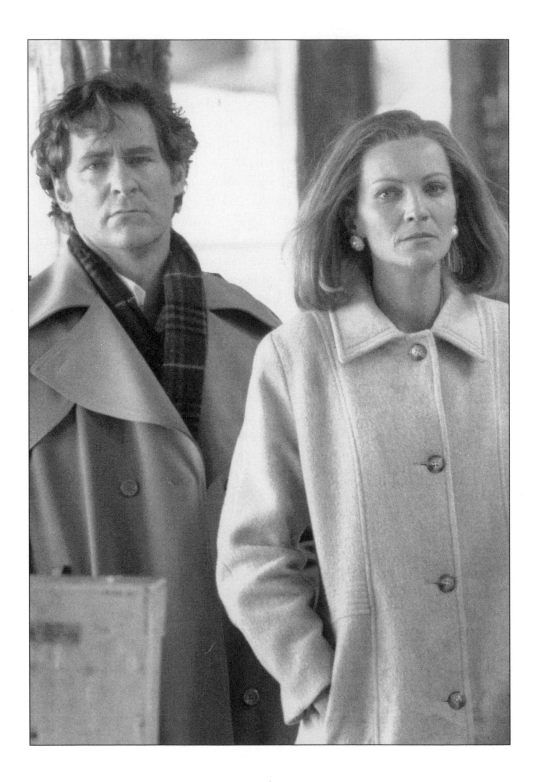

The Ice Storm

Screenplay by
James Schamus

Based on the novel by Rick Moody

Flashforward:

EXT. TRAIN. DARKNESS BEFORE DAWN.   1

Suburban Connecticut, outside of New York City, 1973. The still
after a terrible storm. Trees dripping, their branches torn;
the air warming in the cool blue light just before dawn. The
train lies dark and motionless; a few flashing yellow emergency
lights in front; a work crew removes debris from the track.

INT. TRAIN. PRE-DAWN.   2

Various passengers, huddled uncomfortably, cold, asleep.

On Paul Hood, 15-and-a-half, stoner preppie look, hunched up in
his seat under the faint emergency exit light. He reads his
Fantastic Four comic book by the pale light of the emergency
exit sign.

Suddenly, the lights begin to flicker on and the hum of the
train's engines returns.

The conductor enters the car, blasting forth in his classic
nasal voice.

                    CONDUCTOR
          Good morning ladies and gentle-
          men--

He sounds like a baseball announcer.

                    PASSENGERS
             (mumbling, ad lib)
          What ladies?

                    CONDUCTOR
          -- this train originating at New
          York's Grand Central Station is
          back in service -- next stop will
          be New Canaan, Connecticut. New
          Canaan, Connecticut, next stop!

He moves on to the next car.

The train begins to move.

Paul rubs his elbow against the window and looks out into the
still-dark early morning.

He looks back down at his comic book.

                              (CONTINUED)

CONTINUED: 2

On the comic book: Reed Richards (also known as Stretch) has
zapped his young son with a cosmic ray gun to neutralize the
destructive energy that Annihilus has implanted in him.

The Thing, Medusa, Flame, and Richards' wife Sue Storm look on,
stunned.

        "THEN YOU'VE TURNED HIM INTO A
        <u>VEGETABLE</u>. YOUR OWN <u>SON</u>." "DON'T
        YOU <u>SEE</u>, SUE? HE WAS TOO
        <u>POWERFUL</u>...IF HIS ENERGY HAD
        CONTINUED TO BUILD, HE WOULD HAVE
        DESTROYED THE <u>WORLD</u>!"

Paul looks up again, thinking.

                PAUL
           (voice over)
        In issue number 141 of <u>The</u>
        <u>Fantastic Four</u>, published in
        November 1973, Reed Richards has
        to use his anti-matter weapon on
        his own son, who Annihilus has
        turned into a human atom bomb.
        The problem is that the cosmic
        rays that infused Richards and the
        rest of the Fantastic Four on
        their aborted moon mission have
        made young Franklin a volatile
        mixture of matter and anti-matter.

EXT. TRAIN BRIDGE. PRE-DAWN.   3

The train moves slowly through a suburban, semi-forested
landscape.

                PAUL
          (v.o. cont'd)
        And that's what it is to come from
        a family, if you analyze it
        closely. Your family is kind of
        like your own personal negative
        matter. And that's what dying is
        -- dying is when your family takes
        you back, thus throwing you into
        negative space....

INT. TRAIN. CONT'D.   4

On Paul, as the sun breaks over the horizon. His face glows
warmly in the yellow light. He looks down idly at the comic
book.

                    PAUL
                (v.o. cont'd)
          So it's a paradox -- the closer
          you're drawn back in, the further
          into the void you go. And that's
          what happened the morning of the
          ice storm -- the morning death
          became a member of my family...

EXT. CONRAIL STATION. EARLY MORNING.   5

The train slowly pulls in.

The train doors open, and Paul, weary from the long night,
emerges. He sees his family gathered at the other end of the
platform -- Ben, 40, a bit worse for wear but still retaining
traces of his boyish looks; Elena, 37, distant and elegant even
in her oversized sweater; and Wendy, 14, a sullen suburban
Lolita.

He pauses, regarding them.

They stand, silent, even dignified, awaiting him.

END FLASHFORWARD:
                                        CUT TO:

INT. HOOD HOUSE. LIVING ROOM. DAY.   6

A suburban Connecticut Colonial -- a mixture of a few not-so-
old-money touches and some seventies modular design.

Ben and Elena are mid-argument while she maniacally tidies the
living room.

                    BEN
          You're not saying you want a
          divorce?

                    ELENA
          I'm saying that that's what *you're*
          not saying.

                              (CONTINUED)

CONTINUED: 6

                         BEN
              But all I'm saying is that I don't
              want to get dragged to any more of
              those kooky group therapy things
              --

                         ELENA
              Sure. That's what you say you're
              saying. But what are you *really*
              saying?

                         BEN
              Well, what do you want me to say?

She continues to clean.

                         BEN
              All right, look. If it's that
              important to you, let's give it
              one more shot.

                         ELENA
              You don't really mean it.

                         BEN
              Well at least I said it.

INT. THERAPIST'S OFFICE. EVENING.   7

A woman sobs hysterically as a few other couples, Ben and Elena
among them, sit around in a circle. No one moves. Ben is
sublimely uncomfortable.

                         DR. PASMIER
                    (unctuous)
              Garth, I think what Sue is saying
              here is that she feels oppressed
              by always feeling the need for
              your approval.

                         GARTH
              No she's not -- she's saying I'm a
              piece of shit.

                         DR. PASMIER
              Garth --

                         GARTH
              Just ask her --

                                                      (CONTINUED)

CONTINUED: 7

                         SUE
                    (screaming)
              You piece of shit!

                         GARTH
              I told you so!

Ben just rolls his eyes.

                                        JUMP CUT TO:

INT. THERAPIST'S OFFICE. LATER.   8

Garth and Sue are hugging, crying, and slobbering all over each
other, as the other members of the group gather round them in an
awkward group hug. Dr. Pasmier strokes Garth's hair soothingly.

Ben half participates from the edge of the circle. Elena
glances self-consciously at her husband as she, too, half-
heartedly participates.

                                        JUMP CUT TO:

INT. THERAPIST'S OFFICE. LATER.   9

All seated and calm again.

                         BEN
              So that's what we're evolving into
              -- we're really -- best friends --
              I think. Elena? Right? I think
              we're better friends now than
              we've ever been.

                         MARTY
              In other words you've stopped
              having sex.

                         BEN
              Now wait a sec here Marty --

                         SUE
              We don't have any secrets here,
              Ben. We're here to help each
              other and ourselves -- it's OK not
              to feel OK, because we know you
              really are OK, and --

EXT. PARKING LOT. NIGHT.   10

Ben and Elena walk to the car. He opens her door and walks
around to the driver's side to let himself in.

INT. CAR. NIGHT.   11

Silently, he starts the car and they pull out.

EXT. ST. PETER'S SCHOOL. MORNING.   12

To establish. A typical New England prep school.

INT. ST. PETER'S CLASSROOM. DAY.   13

An English class in progress.

Paul Hood sits blankly, hardly listening, until he hears the
teacher call out.

                    TEACHER
          Who would like to -- Libbets?

Libbets, 15, too earnest and too cute, responds.

                    LIBBETS
          What Dostoevsky is saying here is
          that to be a Christian is to
          choose, because you have to choose
          of your own choice, but since you
          can't choose to be good because
          that would be too rational you
          have to choose to be bad -- it's
          existential.

                    TEACHER
          Thank you Libbets, that's a very
          compelling summary, but --

Paul looks at her, smitten. Marge, Paul's friend, notices his
look.

INT. ST. PETER'S HALLWAY. DAY.   14

As class lets out, Paul accosts Libbets.

                                        (CONTINUED)

CONTINUED: 14

> PAUL
> Um, Libbets. Hey, Dostoevsky, I'm
> also really a fan, and what you
> were saying, you know, have you
> ever read *The Idiot*?

> LIBBETS
> *The Idiot*?

> PAUL
> If you liked *Notes from
> Underground*, you'll love *The
> Idiot*.

> LIBBETS
> (turning to go)
> Great, thanks for the tip.

> PAUL
> (after her)
> *The Idiot*.

INT. ST. PETER'S HALLWAY. DAY.   15

Paul walks with Marge.

> PAUL
> I'm in love with Libbets Casey.

> MARGE
> Yeah, well, you've been in love
> with like every other girl here, I
> was wondering when you'd get
> around to Libbets.

> PAUL
> It's beyond mere physical
> attraction.

> MARGE
> That's good, because I don't think
> Libbets is capable of the sex act.

> PAUL
> Truly? Do speak.

> MARGE
> My diagnosis -- messed in the
> head.
> (more)

(CONTINUED)

CONTINUED: 15

                         MARGE (Cont'd)
          A poor little rich girl -- I mean
          check out the jeans and fur look.
          And lend your ears to this
          brutality. Like her mom and step-
          dad and her step-sisters are going
          to Switzerland to ski over
          Thanksgiving break -- and like
          they didn't invite her!

                         PAUL
          How do you know this shit?

                         MARGE
          They did it last year too. It's
          like traditional or something.
          They've got this humongoid Park
          Ave. apartment and she just holes
          up there with a wad of cash.
                (beat)
          Aren't the hugely wealthy sad?

                         PAUL
                (pause)
          You think Francis is going to beat
          me to the punch here?

                         MARGE
          Since he sleeps with every girl
          you ever show an interest in, why
          don't you just keep your Libbets
          fixation a secret from him?

                         PAUL
                (beat)
          I think I already told him about
          it.

                         MARGE
          Good thinking, Paul.

INT. DORM ROOM. EVENING.   16

Paul enters the room as his roommate, Francis Davenport IV, a
dissolute son of money, is finishing preparing a four-foot-high
bong.

                         PAUL
          I hope you changed the water in
          that bong from last night.

                                                          (CONTINUED)

                         FRANCIS
                    (finishing a hit)
          The water, as you call it, is a
          special mixture of amaretto and
          Ben&Ben blended for just the exact
          chemical interaction with the last
          of our precious Thai stick.

Paul reluctantly walks over and takes a hit. He coughs, spewing
uninhaled smoke.

                         FRANCIS
          Waste not Master Hood -- that was
          $20 for the bag.

                         PAUL
                    (gathering books,
                     papers, almost talking
                     to himself)
          I've been thinking, Francis, you
          know, you are one drug-addled
          elitist freak, and when the
          revolution comes I do not want to
          be lined up with you and shot,
          because you're fucking ripe for
          political reeducation, you know,
          like in the <u>fields</u>.

                         FRANCIS
          Paul, let me enlighten you about
          something. You and I exist on two
          opposite sides of a great
          existential divide, that being
          your pathetic virginity on the one
          hand and my astonishing number of
          sexual conquests on the other.
          You're simply jealous.

A knock at the door.

                         STUDENT
                    (voice off)
          Hood, telephone.

Paul gets up and opens the door.

                         FRANCIS
          And remember, with your erogenous
          zones lubricated as such with the
          mighty herb, beware out there --
          because you drone on like a
          motherfucker when you're stoned.

                                        (CONTINUED)

CONTINUED: (2)   16

                    PAUL
          Flame on, asshole.

INT. DORM HALLWAY. NIGHT.   17

Paul walks to the pay phone at the end of the hall.

                    PAUL
          Hello?

INTERCUT. HOOD HOUSEHOLD. NIGHT.   18

Ben Hood talks on the phone, a drink in his hand.

                    BEN
          Paul?

In the background, we can see Wendy watching Richard Nixon on
TV. Nixon's voice drones on, occasionally filling in the
conversational interstices.

                    PAUL
          Hi, Dad.

                    BEN
          Hey guy. Things OK up there? You
          all right?

                    PAUL
          I'm fine dad.

                    BEN
          Well good. Just confirming.
          You'll be on the 3:50 Wednesday
          afternoon?...Paul, you can't come
          on Thursday because that's already
          Thanksgiving...That's the whole
          point of the holidays, Paul, so
          that you and your sister can mope
          around the house and your mother
          and I can wait on you hand and
          foot while the two of you
          occasionally grunt for more food
          from behind the hair in your
          faces...I know it's hard for you
          to understand, but we actually
          enjoy it and would appreciate --

                              IN THE BACKGROUND:

                              (CONTINUED)

CONTINUED: 18

                              NIXON
                    (on TV, from San
                    Clemente press
                    conference)
               Well, with regard to the questions
               as to why Americans feel we were
               wrong to make the tapes, that is
               not particularly surprising. I
               think that most Americans do not
               like the idea of taping
               conversations and, frankly, it is
               not something that particularly
               appeals to me...

                              BEN
               Good. Thanks guy. Hold on for a
               second.
                    (turning)
               Wendy, you want to say "hi" to
               your brother?

She frowns.

                              BEN
               Come on!

She gets up sullenly and goes to the phone.

                              WENDY
               Charles.

Intercut dorm hall -- another student is waiting behind Paul for
the phone.

                              PAUL
               Charles. Have you been keeping
               out of my shit? Have you
               refrained from entering the sacred
               precincts of my room?

                              WENDY
               I have not touched your sh--
                    (looks at father)
               Stuff. You watching this?

                              PAUL
               Watching what?

                              WENDY
               Nixon, doofus! It's incredible.
               He should be shot.

                                        (CONTINUED)

CONTINUED: (2)   18

                    BEN
              (overhearing)
          Hey, drop the political
          assassination stuff please.

From the kitchen, Elena overhears. She's dressed to go out, but
in the process of making a Kraft macaroni and cheese dinner for
Wendy.

                    WENDY
          He's a liar!
              (still talking more to
               her father than into
               the phone)
          Dean told him on March 21st about
          Kalmback and Hunt, all about the
          payoffs to the Watergate burglars,
          so you tell me where the so-called
          "Dean Report" is, but you can't
          because it doesn't exist, because
          he lied about Haldeman and
          Erlichman and the April 17 tape,
          that's why! Liar!

Ben retreats, going to the wet bar to pour another drink.

                    BEN
              (muttering)
          OK, OK, the defense rests.
              (to Elena in the
               kitchen)
          Want another?

                    ELENA
          No thank you. We should be off.

                    BEN
          Gotcha.

He puts the bottle back down without pouring.

                              INTERCUT BACK TO PAUL:

                    PAUL
              (on the phone)
          Hey Charles. Charles, calm down
          -- I wasn't in on it.

Elena, putting on her coat, comes into the den and gives Wendy a
kiss on the forehead as Wendy mumbles her good-byes to Paul on
the phone.

                              (CONTINUED)

13.

CONTINUED: (3)   18

                         ELENA
              Dinner's on the counter. We'll be
              at the Carvers' -- you know the
              number. (takes the phone from
              Wendy) Paul. Hi. Is there
              anything you'll want, any
              particular kind of food or snack
              or anything we can stock up on?
              ...You're all right? .... OK.
              See you next week. I love you.

Back to Paul. We see that a line has formed for the telephone.
He answers his mother self-consciously.

                         PAUL
              I do you too. I mean, me too.

The kids in line smirk.

Back to Nixon on the TV.

                         NIXON
              We must recognize that one excess
              begets another, and that the
              extremes of violence in the 1960s
              contributed to the extremes of
              Watergate...

On Wendy as she regards the TV, hearing her parents' farewells
as they leave through the front door.

                         BEN
                    (off screen)
              And Wendy! Asleep by 10 - I mean
              it young lady.

Actually, he doesn't sound much like he means it.

EXT. CARVER HOUSE. NIGHT.   19

A large New England Colonial, with a few modern additions and
touches. We hear the sound of dinner chatter.

INT. CARVER DINING ROOM. NIGHT.   20

The kitchen door swings open into the dining room, and Mikey and
Sandy Carver emerge each holding platters of food. Mikey, 15-
and-a-half, lost in space, and Sandy, 14, a sullen and barely
pubescent boy, each have towels draped over their forearms --
they are the evening's "waiters".

                                              (CONTINUED)

They move unsteadily to the table, at which sit their parents
Janey (38, a hard-edged, sharp-witted beauty) and Jim (43, large
and a bit goofy, a genius inventor), together with their guests,
Ben and Elena Hood, and neighbors Dorothy and Ted Franklin.

We jump cut through the evening's conversations, seen mostly
from the furtive POV's of the boys.

> JIM
> It was a benefit for the ACLU or
> something, and Harry Reems himself
> was there --

> DOROTHY
> The man with the -- from Deep
> Throat?

> JIM
> The very one -- something about a
> first amendment defense fund --
> well, I believe in it --

> DOROTHY
> Ted took me to see it.

> JANEY
> Ted, how romantic.

Ted just smiles. The boys' ears tingle imperceptibly.

> DOROTHY
> I have to say, the movie didn't do
> much for me. But being in that
> theater, surrounded by all those
> horny young college boys and
> perverts, there was something in
> the air that --

As this is said, Mikey accidentally spills some wine on Ben.

> BEN
> Hell! -- I mean, no problemo
> "there", Mikey. Here, I --

Janey leans over with her napkin and attempts a cursory wipe of
Ben's pants. Is there a barely noticeable frisson between Ben
and Janey as she removes the napkin? If there is, Elena doesn't
-- or pretends not to -- notice.

                                                   CUT TO:

INT. CARVER DINING ROOM. LATER.   21

The boys, now in pajamas (Sandy's with padded feet, Mikey's a
combination of t-shirt and pj bottoms) are bringing out coffee
and dessert. The adults eye Mikey's handling of the coffee pot
with some nervousness.

                    DOROTHY
          We changed our couples group. Our
          bad luck that all the other
          couples in it were younger and
          better looking, which was terribly
          distracting for poor Ted --

                    TED
          Can't say as my eye didn't wander
          occasionally --

                    DOROTHY
          And hell, if I was going to sit in
          that room while they all talked
          about their sexual problems and
          got little Ted all hot and
          bothered about --

                    TED
          Now we're in some geriatric group
          -- though there's a couple of
          lookers --

                    DOROTHY
               (to Elena)
          But you two are still sticking it
          out with Dr. Pasmier?

                    ELENA
          Actually, Ben decided that, well,
          I mean we both decided --

The room turns to Ben with a slightly accusatory air.

                    BEN
          I just don't see what the appeal
          is. Like you said, Ted, people
          were working themselves up --

                    JIM
          That's the point -- then they go
          home and make up.

                              (CONTINUED)

CONTINUED: 21

                         BEN
              But (puts his arm around Elena,
              who's slightly uncomfortable) --
              Elena and I, we're just not into
              all those histrionics. About the
              only big fight we've had in years
              was about whether or not to stay
              in couple's therapy!

                         JANEY
              And it appears you won.

                         ELENA
              I just thought -- Dr. Pasmier was
              so good with Wendy, when she --

                         DOROTHY
              Your daughter? She's...?

                         ELENA
              With the shoplifting, when she was
              going through that. I had her
              visit with him a few times. And
              she seemed more, well, better --
              So Ben and I talked about it, but
              I guess he's right --

                         JIM
              That's what I like about you two
              -- you seem more like good friends
              than married people.

Janey throws him a glance.

                         DOROTHY
              But then, we still don't know why
              you went to therapy in the first
              place, do we?

Uncomfortable smiles from Ben and Elena.

                                        CUT TO:

INT. CARVER LIVING ROOM. NIGHT.   22

The dinner party has moved to the living room for after-dinner
drinks. Elena remains behind to help Janey pick up the table.
She stacks a plate on top of another.

                         JANEY
              Please don't.

                                        (CONTINUED)

CONTINUED: 22

                         ELENA
                It's not a bother.

                         JANEY
                I insist.
                         (beat)
                Don't touch them.

Elena realizes that there's an edge to Janey's voice.

                         ELENA
                Oh.

                         JANEY
                    (realizing she's gone
                     too far)
                It's really quite all right.

                         ELENA
                Of course.

                                                    CUT TO:

INT. CARVER LIVING ROOM. LATER.   23

The party progresses. Mikey and Sandy lie on their stomachs at
the top of the stairs, out of sight.

                         DOROTHY
                And to think -- they met at a key
                party of all things.

                         ELENA
                A key party?

                         DOROTHY
                You know, it's a California thing.
                That scuzzy husband of hers
                dragged her kicking and screaming
                to one when they were out in LA
                -- you know, the men put their car
                keys in a bowl, and then at the
                end of the evening the women line
                up and fish them out and go home
                with whoever's keys they've got.
                Anyhow, that's how she met this
                Rod person or whatever his name is
                and he's left his wife and she's
                packing for California. Irwin is
                devastated. It's so ironic.

                                                    (CONTINUED)

CONTINUED: 23

                              JANEY
                    Ironic?

                              DOROTHY
                         (caught out)
                    Well, um, yes. Ironic. His name
                    is <u>Rod</u>.

INT. CARVER FRONT HALLWAY. NIGHT.   24

The guests are leaving. The men shake hands, the women kiss,
and the men and women awkwardly peck each others' cheeks.

                              ELENA
                    Thank you Janey.

                              DOROTHY
                    It was lovely!

                              BEN
                    Hey Jim, next time you've got to
                    fill me in on whatever it is
                    you're up to these days -- your
                    inventions and stuff.

                              JIM
                    Will do.

INT. CARVER STAIRWAY. NIGHT.   25

At the top of the stairs, a rather dejected Sandy and Mikey
finish spying on the leave-takings below. Mikey nudges Sandy,
and they silently head back down the upstairs hall.

INT. MIKEY'S ROOM. NIGHT.   26

They enter Mikey's room -- the door has a "nuclear waste --
positively no admittance" sign on it.

As Mikey reaches his bed, he doubles over, groaning, and starts
to make retching noises. He then throws himself onto the bed,
his head leaning over the far side.

Sandy walks over and sees a pile of vomit next to the bed.
Taken aback for a moment, he then reaches forward and picks it
up -- it's fake plastic vomit. He throws it on top of Mikey's
back, but Mikey doesn't take notice.

                              (CONTINUED)

CONTINUED: 26

                              SANDY
                   Stupid!
                         (pause, looking
                          sullenly at Mike's
                          back)
                   Is Wendy Hood your girlfriend?

                              MIKEY
                         (not looking up, but
                          alarmed)
                   Who said so?

                              SANDY
                   No one.

                              MIKEY
                   I don't have a girlfriend.

Mikey returns to his reading -- a copy of *The Sensuous Woman,*
obviously well pawed over. He absent-mindedly picks his nose.
As he flips the pages, a beautiful, almost electrical HUMMING
SOUND begins to fill his ears. He frowns and pauses to listen
to it.

Sandy, who has picked up a balsa wood miniature plane, obviously
doesn't hear it.

Mikey focuses on the plane as Sandy waves it through the air.
Perhaps the hum is the sound of its engines as it soars through
the sky . . .

INT. WENDY'S BEDROOM. NIGHT.   27

There is a large poster of a cartoon version of Richard Nixon --
"Tricky Dick" -- on her wall. Wendy is on the phone to her
friend Beth.

                              WENDY
                   She tried to forge her mom's
                   signature like a total
                   retard...I've done my mom's since
                   like the sixth grade...

She pauses as Beth asks a question.

                              WENDY
                   Who? No way. He's like a big
                   infected whitehead wearing jeans.
                   I wouldn't --

She hears the downstairs door open.

                                        (CONTINUED)

CONTINUED: 27

> WENDY
> (whispering)
> --shit, it's my parents.

She turns her light out.

INT. HOOD UPSTAIRS HALLWAY. NIGHT.   28

Ben and Elena walking past Wendy's room to their bedroom.

> BEN
> You'd think she'd learn how to
> cook a chicken, eh? My drumstick
> was still frozen when you cut
> inside there. I'm probably going
> to get whatever that disease --
> and the Franklins --

He pauses before a hall table, and, with his eyes, traces the
telephone cord under Wendy's room.

> BEN
> Hmm. I knew she'd still be up.
> Watch this --

But Elena simply continues into the master bedroom.

He starts to pull gently on the cord. And continues pulling.
No response for a few seconds. Then:

> WENDY
> (off screen, yelling
> behind her door)
> Dad, stop it!

> BEN
> Get to sleep, young lady -- and I
> mean it.

Wendy opens the door to her room.

> WENDY
> Fascist!

> BEN
> If I were a fascist I would have
> sent you to one of those Southern
> military academies a long time
> ago. Now get to bed.

She slams the door.

(CONTINUED)

CONTINUED: 28

He opens it.

INT. WENDY'S BEDROOM. NIGHT.   29

Ben enters the room, angry.

                    BEN
          Hey!

Wendy jumps into bed and under the covers, pulling them up over
her head. He stands over her, looking down at the crumpled pile
of sheet and blanket.

                    BEN
               (softening)
          Hey, kiddo. Sleep well, huh?

He places his hand where her cheek should be, and caresses the
sheet.

                    WENDY
               (without pulling the
                sheet down, but
                nicely)
          Good-night, Dad.

                    BEN
          Good night, kid.

Ben turns to the door, where he sees a silent Elena standing in
her nightgown, a slight smile on her face.

EXT. NEW CANAAN TRAIN STATION. MORNING.   30

A group of conservatively dressed commuters enter the morning
train for New York City, Ben Hood among them.

INT. TRAIN. MORNING.   31

Ben takes a seat by the window, under the emergency exit sign.

He takes out his *New York Times*, just as Janey Carver sits down
in the seat next to him.

                    BEN
          Janey Carver! I've never seen you
          on the 7:44.

                    JANEY
          Good morning, Ben.

                         (CONTINUED)

                    BEN
          You haven't gotten a job, or --

                    JANEY
          Passport office. Didn't you hear
          Jimmy rant on about it last week?
          He wants us all to go to Africa
          this summer. The shit.

                    BEN
          Sounds exciting to me.

                    JANEY
          Well then I'll ask Jimmy to take
          you in my place. It's a photo
          safari, so you can take pictures
          of the animals instead of killing
          them.

                    BEN
          I guess that's more ...
          ecological.

                    JANEY
          Is your office mid-town or
          downtown?

                    BEN
          Mid-town. Park and 52nd.

                    JANEY
          Near the Mayflower Hotel?

                    BEN
          I think so. Uh...

                    JANEY
          I hear they have a good
          restaurant. I've just had
          breakfast but you know I'm already
          thinking about lunch.

She picks up a piece of Ben's paper and starts to read it.

EXT. MANHATTAN OFFICE BUILDING. DAY.   32

A nondescript, cleanly "modern" building. Engraved on the
doors: "Shackley and Schwimmer, Securities Brokerage --
Established 1964"

INT. SHACKLEY AND SCHWIMMER CONFERENCE ROOM. DAY.   33

Ben sits among a small group of men, which includes George
Clair, mid-thirties, unctuously handsome.

                    GEORGE
          You see Mr. Shackley, that's what
          I'm getting at -- I believe
          Forrester Industries should reduce
          its cash position -- especially
          during this period of stagflation.
          I think we can show them much
          better returns, and in the process
          earn some beefier commissions,
          if --

                    BEN
          -- But George, Mr. Shackley, I'd
          like to pause for a second, and
          ask, if it's ok, what, exactly, is
          stagflation.

                    GEORGE
          Uh, Ben --

                    BEN
          We know it's a mixture of
          inflation and stagnation. Right.
          So how should we in the securities
          industry accommodate it? Well --
          and I hope I'm not out of bounds
          here -- let's for a moment think
          of the money supply as a large
          male organ, continuously
          inflating, and yet, the societal
          vaginal cavity simply wants more.
          As the vicious circle of higher
          returns without real satisfaction
          continues, the money-organ may
          seem to be in demand, but in fact
          even the most inflated capital is
          unwanted. This is why I suggest
          that while Forrester may be lured
          by the promise of high returns, it
          should still fantasize, so to
          speak, about the safe harbor of
          capital appreciation.

The aging boss nods agreement.

                    SHACKLEY
               (more or less mumbling)
          Brilliant, brilliant.

George Clair just grins meanly.

INT. BEN HOOD'S OFFICE./ EXT. HALL. DAY.   34

Ben is gathering papers, readying to leave. He looks up to see
George Clair in his doorway.

                    GEORGE
          Hey there Benjie, you're becoming
          quite the in-house philosopher.
          When do you have time to think up
          all that stuff -- Shackley sure
          eats it up.

INTERCUT. HALL IN FRONT OF BEN HOOD'S OFFICE.

We see that Clair is deftly flirting with Hood's attractive
secretary as she is sitting in the cubicle beside the door to
his office. She looks up coyly at Clair, hidden for the moment
from Ben's view.

Ben comes out of his office, pulling on his coat. Ben vaguely
senses what's transpiring between Clair and his secretary.

                    BEN
          George, I'm just trying to get a
          global view of things -- can't
          just look at the small picture.

There's an obvious rivalry between the two of them.

                    GEORGE
          Right on, Ben. But when the old
          man retires, I bet you're going to
          have to come up with a new routine
          -- Schwimmer doesn't seem too into
          your macroeconomic thing.

                    BEN
          Thanks for the tip, George.

                    GEORGE
          No charge, Ben. Hey, you heading
          out just a little bit early today?

                    BEN
          Got a meeting uptown.

                    GEORGE
             (already moving off)
          Right on.

                              (CONTINUED)

CONTINUED: 34

                         BEN
              Up the organization!
                   (then, to himself)
              Bastard.

The secretary pretends not to hear.

INT. BOOK STORE. DAY.   35

Elena browses the self-help section. A longish-haired, slightly
gone-to-seed, but still handsome clergyman pauses next to her.
He's wearing an ecclesiastical collar and bell-bottoms.

He pulls out a copy of *Me, Myself and I*, glancing again at
Elena.

                         PHILIP
              Elena. Elena Hood, am I right?

                         ELENA
              Yes.

                         PHILIP
              Reverend Edwards. Philip Edwards.
              You came by and checked out the
              congregation a couple of times
              last year.

                         ELENA
              Yes, it was -- I ended up --

                         PHILIP
                   (smiling)
              No need to make excuses -- we're
              not for everyone, I know. (beat)
              But I did think, for a time, that
              you might be someone -- What I
              mean is that you didn't seem to
              think what we were trying to do is
              laughable, like some of your
              fellow citizens around hereabouts.

                         ELENA
              No, I didn't think it laughable at
              all, I --

                         PHILIP
                   (gesturing to her
                   books)
              Perhaps you find in books what I
              try to find in people.

                                             (CONTINUED)

CONTINUED: 35

                         ELENA
                  (a pained smile)
            That sounds vaguely like an
            insult.

                         PHILIP
            Oh my. I'm sorry, I didn't mean
            it that way at all. Perhaps I
            meant it simply as a -- a
            provocation.

She thinks about it, and smiles again.

EXT. NEW CANAAN HIGH SCHOOL FIELD. DAY.   36

A cool gray afternoon. A group of boys are playing flag
football on the field, while two groups of girls are gathered
underneath the bleachers at either end, warily smoking
cigarettes.

Wendy, Beth, and a couple of other girls are gathered in one
group.

                         BETH
                  (referring to one of
                   the girls gathered in
                   the other group)
            She said you licked Dave
            Brewster's weenie in the third
            floor bathroom.

                         WENDY
            She's a liar. I wouldn't touch
            Dave Brewster's dick if you paid
            me. It's probably crawling with
            v.d. after he put it in her, which
            he did.

The conversation peters out at this point, as the two groups of
girls give each other the hairy eyeball from afar.

Wendy looks through from beneath the bleacher seats onto the
field where the boys are playing.

A group of boys break from a huddle, Mikey among them.

The quarterback takes the hike and Mikey runs out for a pass.
As he runs, his breathing increases in volume, filling his ears,
and transforming into the HUMMING SOUND he'd heard before.

The quarterback spots him and throws a long one.

                                        (CONTINUED)

CONTINUED: 36

He runs in an oblivion of beautiful white sound.

The ball drops next to him as he continues, in a world of his
own, to run.

Suddenly, the humming ends and he stops and turns around, to see
all of the other kids just standing there looking at him. One
of them makes a pot-smoking gesture, as if that's the
explanation.

                    MIKEY
               (as he returns to the
               group, ball in hand)
          Did anybody hear that?

The other kids snicker. Wendy looks on, and catches Mikey's eye
for a fleeting moment.

                    WENDY
          I gotta go.

She takes hold of her bicycle and pushes off.

INT. COFFEE SHOP. DAY.   37

Elena and Philip are seated at a booth.

                    PHILIP
          It's been a tremendously
          transformative year -- maybe a
          little controversial, of course,
          but we're breaking down the old
          Unitarian barriers --

                    ELENA
          I suppose my reluctance was the
          group aspect of it -- I've never
          been much of a joiner, although I
          still consider myself a somewhat
          religious person --

                    PHILIP
          Well, I of course flatter myself
          that our church is not exactly
          what most people would call
          organized religion -- at times
          it's the disorganization that's
          liberating -- and of course I've
          begun to minister much more in
          what one might call therapeutic
          environments, in small groups, and
          one on one, couples --

CONTINUED: 37

Elena looks outside the window, and sees Wendy speed past on her
bicycle.

                    ELENA
               (cutting him off)
          My daughter. I haven't been on a
          bike for years.
               (still not really
                looking at him)
          When was the last time you rode a
          bike?

                    PHILIP
               (a bit taken aback by
                the abrupt topic
                change)
          They say you never forget.

                    ELENA
               (jarred back to his
                presence)
          Forget what?

There's something mildly flirtatious and perhaps a bit sinister
about his manner.

                    PHILIP
          Forget how to ride a bike.

Silence.

                    ELENA
          No, of course you don't, you're
          right.

EXT. FIVE AND DIME STORE. DAY.   38

Wendy pulls her bike up to the back, locks it, and walks in.

INT. FIVE AND DIME STORE. DAY.   39

Wendy moves with a certain amount of stealth through the aisles,
arriving at the candy selection.

She looks around.

She takes a package of Twinkies and slips them into the
oversized pockets of her painter's pants.

                              (CONTINUED)

CONTINUED: 39

She turns around, and her breath goes out of her -- an OLD WOMAN
has been watching her shoplift. The woman looks sadly at her,
but says nothing. Wendy slowly walks past her and out the back
door of the store. The woman looks on.

EXT. FIVE AND DIME STORE. DAY.   40

As she walks her bike onto the sidewalk, Wendy comes across
Sandy.

                    SANDY
          Hey, Wendy.

                    WENDY
          Hey, Sandy.

                    SANDY
          Mikey was looking for you.

                    WENDY
          Yeah? See ya.

She pushes off on her bike.

Sandy gazes after her. He takes his G.I. Joe out of his coat
pocket, and points it at her.

                    SANDY
          Bam.

EXT. SUBURBAN STREETS. DAY.   41

Wendy flies along on her bike. It's a desolately beautiful fall
day.

EXT. SILVER MEADOWS PSYCHIATRIC INSTITUTE. DAY.   42

Wendy rides by the front gates of the posh grounds of the
private psychiatric clinic. A security guard leans against a
booth.

Once a bit past the gate, she gets off her bike and walks it
into a grove of trees near the front drive.

EXT. SILVER MEADOWS. DAY.   43

Mikey is waiting amid the trees next to his bike as Wendy
arrives.

                                                   (CONTINUED)

CONTINUED: 43

           MIKEY
Want some gum?

           WENDY
Sure.
    (pulling them out of
    her pocket)
Twinkie?

           MIKEY
    (opens his mouth,
    displaying the gum on
    his tongue)
I'm chewing.

She puts the Twinkies back, and pops the gum in her mouth.

They stand together chewing.

           WENDY
    (after a pause)
Did you tell Sandy?

           MIKEY
Tell Sandy? What?

Wendy doesn't say anything.

           MIKEY
You didn't tell him either, did
you?

EXT. SILVER MEADOWS SWIMMING POOL. DAY. 44

The wind is picking up and the light is fading. Mikey and Wendy
climb the fence around the pool, which is empty and half-covered
in dead leaves and twigs.

They climb down into the concrete recess and walk into the deep
end, leaning against the far wall of the pool.

They each matter-of-factly take their gum out and put it behind
their ears.

They begin not so much to kiss as to place their tongues in each
others' mouths.

We see them from high above the pool. As the dead leaves swirl
lightly around them, Mikey gropes under Wendy's poncho.

EXT. CARVER HOUSE. DAY.   45

To establish.

INT. CARVER GUEST ROOM. DAY.   46

A couple are in the final throes of lovemaking. We see Janey
Carver's face, more or less enjoying the proceedings. The man
gives a final heave and groan, and rolls off to reveal himself
to be -- Ben Hood.

                              JUMP CUT TO:

INT. CARVER GUESTROOM. LATER.   47

Janey smokes a cigarette. Ben is babbling.

                    BEN
          We were golfing, and you know,
          golfing to me is something I'm
          supposed to enjoy, and I was on
          the goddamn golf team in college,
          so it's something one would assume
          I do well -- I used to do well --
          but basically these days golfing
          for me is like hoeing, or plowing.

Janey smiles briefly at this.

                    BEN
          It's like farming. I am basically
          chewing up large tracts of
          expensively landscaped scenery
          with overpriced sticks, and George
          Clair has obviously, in the mere
          two years since he joined the
          firm, he has obviously been taking
          secret lessons with a golf pro,
          and I bet the entirety of his
          disposable income has been devoted
          to humiliating me on the golf
          course. And the guy talks --
          nonstop -- throughout the
          entirety of the miserable 18 holes
          -- on topics that are the supposed
          domain of my department --

                    JANEY
          Ben--

                              (CONTINUED)

                    BEN
    Yeah?

                    JANEY
       (gently)
    You're boring me. I have a
    husband. I don't particularly
    feel the need for another.

He takes a deep breath.

                    BEN
    You have a point there. That's a
    very good point. We're having an
    affair. Right. An explicitly
    sexual relationship. Your needs.
    My needs. You're absolutely
    right.

                    JANEY
    You should probably get dressed.
    The boys will be home soon.

                    BEN
    Gotcha.

She wraps a blanket around herself and gets up.

EXT. BACK OF CARVER HOUSE. EVENING.   48

Ben cautiously walks out the back door and heads for the side
gate.

INT. HOOD KITCHEN. EVENING.   49

Wendy enters the house as Elena is finishing supper
preparations.

                    WENDY
    Hi mom.

                    ELENA
    Hi Wendy.

Without waiting for instructions, Wendy starts pulling out
plates and silverware and setting the table.

                    ELENA
    I saw you on your bike today.

(CONTINUED)

                         WENDY
          With Mikey?

                         ELENA
          Who?

                         WENDY
          Nobody.

                         ELENA
          Mikey Carver?

                         WENDY
          We were just riding around.

Elena takes this in.

                         ELENA
          Well, you looked very -- free --
          when I saw you.

Wendy continues setting the table.

                         ELENA
          Weightless almost -- as if I were
          seeing my own memories of being a
          girl. There was something
          internal about it.

                         WENDY
          Mom. Are you ok?

                         ELENA
          Wendy, of course. I'm sorry. You
          must think I'm ripe to be checked
          into Silver Meadows.

                         WENDY
          You're not a psycho!

                         ELENA
          The people at Silver Meadows
          aren't psychos.

                         WENDY
          I know. They're rich drug addicts
          and celebrities. When I saw James
          Taylor there, and --

                                        (CONTINUED)

CONTINUED: (2)   49

                    ELENA
          We've been through this, Wendy --
          James Taylor was actually at that
          clinic up near Boston.

                    WENDY
          Well, I saw what I saw, and if you
          don't want to believe me --

                    ELENA
          Oh, Wendy.

Wendy frowns.

                    WENDY
          They need the money for my band
          uniform at school.

                    ELENA
          I thought you quit the band -- I
          never hear you practice anymore.

                    WENDY
          I don't really need to practice.
          I just play a few notes, you know,
          so I thought maybe I'd stay in.

                    ELENA
          Well, I'm sure your father and I
          would love to hear what you're
          playing these days. Maybe after
          dinner.

INT. HOOD LIVING ROOM. NIGHT.   50

Ben and Elena take their seats on the sofa. Wendy stands before
them holding an enormous trombone, with a music stand and sheet
music in front of her.

She puffs a series of seemingly disconnected notes in waltz
time.

When she's done, she looks up from the sheet music to her
parents.

They applaud.

                    BEN
          Can't wait to see how it fits in
          with all the other instruments.

                                              (CONTINUED)

CONTINUED: 50

Elena gives him a look.

INT. HOOD KITCHEN. NIGHT.   51

Elena is sorting through bills and writing checks at the kitchen
table. Ben comes in and fills a glass with ice.

                    ELENA
          The Halfords have invited us again
          this year.

                    BEN
          You want to go?

                    ELENA
          What do you think?

                    BEN
          Well, it is a neighborhood
          tradition.

He comes up behind her, looks down at the checkbook.

                    BEN
          I'm, uh, going to bed.

                    ELENA
          So early?

                    BEN
          Rough day. Good night.

He leans over and kisses her on the cheek. She sniffs.

                    ELENA
          Is that a new aftershave?

He recoils a bit.

                    BEN
          Oh yeah. Musk, or something. You
          like it?

                    ELENA
          Hmm. Good night.

He walks uncertainly from the room. She watches him go. Does
she know?

INT. MIKEY'S ROOM. NIGHT.   52

Mikey is painfully at work writing an English essay. Sandy
comes to the door with a geometry textbook.

                    SANDY
    Mikey?

                    MIKEY
    Yeah?

                    SANDY
    Geometry?

                    MIKEY
    Sure, anything but this English.

Sandy puts the open textbook in front of him.

                    SANDY
    Why are you so good at math but
    not in English?

                    MIKEY
    I'm not good at math. Just
    geometry.

He looks at the book.

                    MIKEY
        (drawing out his
         examples on a piece of
        paper)
    It's like, you know when they say
    "two squared"? And you think it
    means 2 times 2, equals 4? But
    really they really mean a square.
    A square with a side of two. And
    the area of the square is four.
    Like every time you use the word,
    like squared, or cubed, it's
    really space, it's not numbers,
    it's space. And it's perfect
    space, but only in your head,
    because you can't draw a perfect
    square, like in the material
    world, but in your mind, you can
    have perfect space.
        (pause)
    You know?

As Mikey goes on, we see his geometric doodles, and hear faintly
the HUMMING SOUND under his voice.

                (CONTINUED)

37.

CONTINUED: 52

                    SANDY
          Yeah. But I just need some help
          with my homework.

A knock at the door. Jim stands in the doorway with a suitcase
in his hand.

                    JIM
          Hey guys, I'm back.

                    MIKEY
               (honestly confused)
          You were gone?

Sandy looks at Mikey as if pondering a lost cause.

                    JIM
               (a look of
               disappointment)
          Yeah, Mikey. Yep, I was in
          Houston, working on some great new
          ideas about silicon, which comes
          from sand, very conductive. How
          you guys doing? How's school?

Mikey's still flustered.

                    MIKEY
          Uh, I dunno. OK, I guess.

                    JIM
          Hmm. All right!

He walks off.

                    SANDY
          You really didn't notice? Man,
          he's been gone for three days.

INT. CARVER BEDROOM. NIGHT.   53

Janey is reading, still dressed, on the bed. She nods to Jim as
he enters with his suitcase.

                    JANEY
          Good trip?

He nods and puts his suitcase down, then sits heavily on the
side of the bed.

                              (CONTINUED)

CONTINUED: 53

                    JIM
                (as he sits)
         You bet.

It turns out it's a water bed, and his weight creates a wave
that nearly pushes Janey off her edge of the bed.

                    JANEY
         Jesus, Jim!

                    JIM
                (jumping up, which only
                 creates another wave)
         Sorry honey. Hell, we've got to
         trade this thing in for a normal
         bed.

                    JANEY
         Just be careful.

                    JIM
                (as he begins to
                 unpack)
         You notice anything with Mikey
         lately? The kid seemed a little
         out of it tonight, eh?

                    JANEY
         Tonight? Jim, he's been out of it
         since he was born.

                    JIM
         Hell, I guess he takes after me,
         huh?

He laughs to himself.

She gives him a look.

INT. COFFEE SHOP. DAY.   54

Elena and Philip Edwards are having coffee again.

                    PHILIP
         In many ways, the church-bound
         tradition of the father, son, and
         holy ghost is simply a version of
         the parent-child-adult triad
         within us all. It's a primitive
         set of symbols for our inner
         psychology.

                                        (CONTINUED)

                        ELENA
          You're saying that Christ is the
          child, and --

                        PHILIP
          -- And God the angry parent, and
          the Spirit the hope of an
          integrated adult self.

                        ELENA
          All well and good -- But tell me
          again what it is exactly that you
          believe in?

                        PHILIP
          You ask what the point is?

                        ELENA
          That's right.

                        PHILIP
          Self-realization. Ministering to
          help people reach their fullest
          potential. Would you believe me
          if I told you I want you to see
          yourself reach your fullest
          potential and self-realization?

                        ELENA
                 (pause)
          I would say it sounds like you're
          trying to get me into bed.

                        PHILIP
          If that's a potential you see
          yourself fulfilling...I mean...
          (flustered) My, I sound a bit --

                        ELENA
          I'm sorry. That was stupid of me.
          I didn't mean to be so rude.

                        PHILIP
          You weren't. You actually, for
          some reason, you have the effect
          of making me feel just a tiny bit
          ashamed of myself.

                        ELENA
          But not too ashamed.

                                        (CONTINUED)

                    PHILIP
                 (smiling)
        Now you are being rude.

                    ELENA
        And you're still trying to get me
        into bed.

                    PHILIP
        Ouch.

Just then, Dorothy Franklin passes by their table, a smirk
firmly implanted on her face.

                    DOROTHY
        Hello you two. Am I barging in on
        some kind of religious study
        group? Elena, you look marvelous.
        Will I see you and Ben at the
        Halford's?

                    ELENA
        I suppose we'll make an
        appearance.

                    DOROTHY
        And Reverend Edwards? Did you
        make the list?

                    PHILIP
                 (laughing)
        I believe so Mrs. Franklin.

                    DOROTHY
        With the two of you there it will
        be positively a revival! I'm off!

She scurries out of the coffee shop.

                    PHILIP
        I'm afraid she's something of a
        gossip, isn't she?

                    ELENA
                 (gathering her things
                  to go)
        I'm afraid people around here
        provide her with quite a bit to
        gossip about. (getting up) Take
        care.

                                        (CONTINUED)

                    PHILIP
             (watching her go)
      That I will indeed.

INT. CLASSROOM. DAY.   55

Mikey is reading his English paper before the class.

                    MIKEY
      Because of molecules we are
      connected to the outside world
      from our bodies. Like when you
      smell things, because when you
      smell a smell it's not really a
      smell, it's a part of the object
      that has come off of it --
      molecules. So when you smell
      something bad, it's like in a way
      you're eating it. This is why
      you should not really smell
      things, in the same way that you
      don't eat everything in the world
      around you -- because as a smell,
      it gets inside of you. So the
      next time you go into the bathroom
      after someone else has been there,
      remember what kinds of molecules
      you are in fact eating.

An embarrassed silence.

INT. SCHOOL MUSIC ROOM. DAY.   56

Band practice. The New Canaan High School band plays a wind
version of a popular rock tune.

In front, there's Wendy, in halter top and hip-hugging bell
bottoms, incongruously blowing away on her trombone -- this
being her one stab at extracurricular activities.

In the flute section directly behind her is Sandy, piping away
on a tiny piccolo. He sits on a riser slightly elevated above
her.

He directs downward at Wendy a protracted regard, a look of
intense concentration on his face.

                    (CONTINUED)

CONTINUED: 56

SANDY'S POV:

Wendy's backside, her pants pushed outward in the back,
affording Sandy a libido-charged view of the top of her bum
crack.

Push in on a close-up of this cherished abstract landscape, then
back to Sandy's furrowed face.

INT. HOOD DEN. DAY.   57

Elena sits in a yoga pose. She opens her eyes and lets her
limbs relax.

INT. HOOD GARAGE. DAY.   58

Elena enters the garage from the kitchen and turns the light on.

She finds an old bicycle and pulls it out.

EXT. SUBURBAN STREETS. DAY.   59

Elena rides her bike into town, infused with the girlish sense
of freedom she imagined for her daughter.

Suddenly, there's a pop -- a tire is blown out. She slows down
and gets off the bike.

EXT. SUBURBAN STREETS. LATER.   60

She walks with the bike, as a station wagon slows near her. The
driver's side window rolls open. It's Janey Carver.

                    JANEY
          Need a lift?

INT. JANEY'S CAR. DAY.   61

Elena sits in the passenger seat. The two women are obviously
uncomfortable with each other.

Silence.

                    ELENA
          Thanks again. For the dinner.

                                        (CONTINUED)

CONTINUED: 61

                    JANEY
          Thanks for eating it. I don't
          know why I even pretend I can
          cook.

                    ELENA
          I used to know how to cook.

                    JANEY
          It's not like we're too busy.

They smile, barely.

                    ELENA
          I'm thinking of going back to
          school.

                    JANEY
          Social work?

                    ELENA
          How'd you know?

                    JANEY
          Educated guess.

                    ELENA
          I'm that predictable? No, you
          don't have to answer that. It's
          just that with the kids almost
          grown --

                    JANEY
          You don't have to apologize. I'm
          too much of a cynic. You actually
          seem to be trying to figure things
          out. Don't mind me.

She pulls the car over.

EXT. FIVE AND DIME STORE. DAY.   62

Janey's car pulls to the curb.

INT. JANEY'S CAR. CONT'D.

                    JANEY
          Here you are.

                              (CONTINUED)

CONTINUED: 63

                    ELENA
              (opening her door)
         Thanks for the lift. If the
         bike's any bother--

                    JANEY
         None at all. I'll leave it in
         front of your garage. Happy
         Thanksgiving.

EXT. FIVE AND DIME. CONT'D.   64

Elena watches the car pull away. She turns and walks into the
store.

INT. FIVE AND DIME. DAY.   65

Elena moves through the aisles, putting various sundries into a
basket.

She pauses in front of the lipsticks.

She picks up a lipstick, looks at it, then quietly places it in
her pocketbook. She puts the basket down on an empty aisle
shelf.

We see her reflection in the security mirror above the aisle, as
she quickly exits the store.

The middle-aged lady behind the counter watches her leave.

EXT. FIVE AND DIME. DAY.   66

In a wide shot, from across the street, we see Elena leave the
store, followed by the shopkeeper who runs behind her and taps
her on the shoulder. They converse for a minute, and Elena is
accompanied back into the store.

Through the store windows we see her take the lipstick out of
her purse. She's obviously distraught -- offering to pay,
talking quickly, etc. The shopkeeper is holding a telephone, not
yet decided on whether to call her in.

                              (CONTINUED)

CONTINUED: 66

                         PAUL
                    (voice over)
          To find yourself in the Negative
          Zone, as the Fantastic Four often
          do, means that all everyday
          assumptions are inverted -- even
          the invisible girl herself becomes
          visible, and so she loses the last
          semblance of her power.

EXT. TRAIN. DAY.   67

As it moves through the gray afternoon landscape.

INT. TRAIN. DAY.   68

Close on images from The Fantastic Four.

          "HERE IN THE NEGATIVE ZONE, HIS
          POWERS ARE HALVED. WE CAN DO
          NOTHING BUT WAIT...AND PRAY" "BUT
          WHAT ABOUT FRANKLIN? HE'LL BE
          KILLED!"

Paul sits reading on his way home.

EXT. CARVER HOUSE. DAY.   69

Janey pulls up in the driveway. As she gets out of the car, she
hears a small explosion from the back of the house.

EXT. CARVER BACKYARD. DAY.   70

Janey comes around the back to discover Sandy stuffing a model
airplane with m-80 firecrackers. He lights them and runs back a
safe distance. The plane explodes, its wreckage joining the
debris from a few other dolls, models, and toys.

                         JANEY
          Sandy!

Sandy looks up -- busted.

Janey marches over to him.

                                        (CONTINUED)

CONTINUED: 70

                         JANEY
            You little idiotic prick, you
            could blow yourself fucking sky
            high with all this demented crap.

Sandy looks on the verge of tears. She softens and bends down
to him.

                         JANEY
                    (sighing)
            Hey.
                    (picking up the
                     firecrackers)
            I'll take this stuff.

                         SANDY
            You going to tell dad?

                         JANEY
            Would it matter?
                    (sees something else
                     lying on the ground)
            And what's that?

                         SANDY
                    (sniffling)
            You know, it's the whip -- the one
            uncle Frank got me from Mexico.

                         JANEY
            It's not packed with explosives,
            is it?

                         SANDY
            No!

                         JANEY
                    (going into the house)
            Play with the whip.

INT. CARVER LIVING ROOM. DAY.   71

Mikey and Wendy are in front of the TV, watching a rerun of
Divorce Court.

                         JANEY
            Oh. Hi, Wendy.

                         WENDY
            Hi, Mrs. Carver.

                                                    (CONTINUED)

>   JANEY
>   Mikey, have you heard the
>   explosions coming from the
>   backyard?
>   (he stares blankly at
>   her)
>   Do you know what Sandy's been up
>   to?

>   MIKEY
>   (honestly oblivious, as
>   usual)
>   I dunno.

She pauses, then walks into the kitchen.

EXT. CARVER BACKYARD. DAY.   72

Sandy flicks his enormous whip in the direction of a small bush.

One by one, he snaps off its leaves.

INT. CARVER KITCHEN. DAY.   73

Janey hauls a turkey out of a bag and into the fridge.

INT. CARVER LIVING ROOM. DAY.   74

Mikey and Wendy are still in front of the TV.

Janey comes in again and looks at them.

>   JANEY
>   Excuse me. Don't you kids have
>   homework?

>   MIKEY AND WENDY
>   (without looking up, in
>   unison)
>   Thanksgiving break.

She walks out of the room again.

Sandy comes in, whip in hand, looks over at Mikey and Wendy,
then walks over to them, and, without a word, slumps down beside
them and watches the TV.

EXT. TOWN STREET. DAY.   75

Elena walks unsteadily, pausing to rest against a brick wall.
She takes a deep breath, then walks to a corner where a local
taxi station wagon sits idling. She gestures to the driver, who
beckons her in.

INT. CARVER LIVING ROOM. DAY.   76

Later, Sandy, Mikey, and Wendy still mentally devolve in front
of the TV, but with various junk food detritus surrounding them
and a different show, a rerun of the original *Highway Patrol*.

Sandy wanders off.

                              CUT TO:

INT. CARVER LIVING ROOM / STAIRS / BATHROOM. LATER.   77

Wendy gets up, goes upstairs, and wanders down the hall to the
bathroom.

She gets to the door just as Sandy gets there from the opposite
direction.

                    WENDY
          After you.

Sandy hesitantly opens the door, as Wendy still hovers by it.

                    SANDY
          Well, you can....

                    WENDY
          Hey Sandy, what were you blowing
          up out there? Your mom was pretty
          p.o.'d.

                    SANDY
          All my model planes.

                    WENDY
          The ones you built?

                    SANDY
          They were old. And they couldn't
          fly anyhow. I'm going to get a
          radio-controlled airplane at
          Christmas, and then I'll stuff it
          full of m-80s and fly it into Mrs.
          Burgess's English class and blow
          it up.

                              (CONTINUED)

CONTINUED: 77

                         WENDY
          I have to go to the bathroom.

                         SANDY
          Yeah.

But he stays put, unaware it seems that he's blocking the
doorway.

Wendy looks around -- no one in sight.

                         WENDY
          I'll show you mine if you show me
          yours.

Sandy goes wide-eyed, and almost against his will backs into the
bathroom like a feather.

INT. CARVER LIVING ROOM. DAY.   78

Mikey looks up from the TV, wondering where Wendy is. He eats
another Pringle.

INT. CARVER BATHROOM. DAY.   79

Wendy flips up her dress for Sandy.

He slowly unzips, his hand unsteady. We can tell from the look
on Wendy's face that she's feeling a bit sorry for the little
guy.

Suddenly Sandy turns beet red, and bursts into tears.

                         SANDY
          What do you want?! What do you
          want? Get out! Get out of here!

The door flips open -- and Janey Carver appears.

                         JANEY
                    (sizing up the
                     situation)
          Shit.

INT. MASTER BEDROOM. DAY.   80

Janey is giving Wendy a lecture.

                              (CONTINUED)

CONTINUED: 80

> JANEY
> A person's body is his temple,
> Wendy. This body is your first
> and last possession. Now as your
> own parents have probably told
> you, in adolescence our bodies
> tend to betray us. That's why, in
> Samoa and in other developing
> nations, adolescents are sent out
> into the woods, unarmed, and they
> don't come back until they've
> learned a thing or two. Do you
> understand?

INT. CARVER HOUSE DOORWAY. DAY.   81

Wendy is led to the door by Mrs. Carver.

Wendy trades a glance with a sullen Mikey, who sits in the
living room pretending to ignore her.

EXT. STREET. DAY.   82

Wendy walks her bike with the wind in her face.

Mikey rides up alongside her on his bike.

She doesn't look at him.

Trying to stay on his bike, but moving slowly, he wobbles,
nearly falling off.

> MIKEY
> I don't ever want to see you.

> WENDY
> Then why'd you come after me?

EXT. HOOD HOUSE. DAY.   83

The taxi pulls up. Elena gets out and pays the driver.

INT. HOOD KITCHEN. DAY.   84

Ben is in front of the open freezer, trying to get something
out. He hears Elena come in the front door.

(CONTINUED)

CONTINUED: 84

                         BEN
              Elena. I need some help here if
              this thing's gonna defrost by
              tomorrow.

She comes up and together they tug and pull until they succeed
in extracting a large, frozen turkey. As they pull it out, it
slips from their hands and, after a dull thump, slides along the
floor.

They smile.

Elena bends over to pick it up. Ben observes her. She notices
his look.

                         BEN
              Here.

He goes over and picks up the turkey, placing it in the sink.
He looks back at her and notices her vaguely distraught look.

                         BEN
              You all right there?

                         ELENA
              Oh. Sure, I -- Did you remember
              to pick up the cranberry sauce?

                         BEN
              Um, yes.

They stand together, his concern and her vulnerability forming
an awkward attraction between them.

                         ELENA
              Because you like it on your turkey
              sandwiches.

                         BEN
              I do. I'm -- are you...?

                         ELENA
              I...I think I...

                         BEN
                   (pause)
              You know Elena, I've been
              thinking --

                         ELENA
              Ben, maybe no talking right now?
              If you start talking, you're going
              to --

                                        (CONTINUED)

CONTINUED: (2)   84

She kisses him as if she needs him.

INT. HOOD HALLWAY. DAY.   85

Ben and Elena enter their bedroom. Elena closes the door
quietly behind her.

INT. HOOD BEDROOM. DAY.   86

Ben and Elena undress shyly.

They make love. Elena's face is almost fearful.

                                        CUT TO:

INT. HOOD BEDROOM. LATER.   87

Elena and Ben lie in bed side by side in the pale afternoon
light.

                    BEN
          Wow. You kind of forget what
          you're missing...

He gets up and starts to get dressed.

                    BEN
          I should probably be getting
          going, to get Paul.

He smells the armpits of the shirt he's putting on.

                    BEN
          Yikes -- I was hoping to wear this
          thing to the Halford's Friday.

He looks at Elena, and realizes she's started to cry.

                    BEN
          Hey. Elena?

                    ELENA
          It's nothing.

                    BEN
          What? What is it?

                    ELENA
          That shirt?

                                        (CONTINUED)

                         BEN
          What?

                         ELENA
          Leave it -- I'll wash it for you.

He looks at her ruefully.

EXT. HOOD STREET. DAY.   88

Wendy walks and Mikey rides along.

                         WENDY
          You have to follow me?

                         MIKEY
          I dunno. I --

They're now in front of the Hood's house.

EXT. HOOD HOUSE. DAY.   89

Ben exits the house in a rush, and sees Wendy and Mikey on the
street in front.

                         BEN
          Hey, there Mikey, how's business?

                         MIKEY
                    (tripping off of his
                     bike)
          Business? Uh, I dunno.

Ben grimaces, fiddles for his car keys.

As Mikey remounts and rides off, Wendy passes her father on the
driveway.

                         BEN
          I'm picking up Paul at the station
          -- want to come?

                         WENDY
          Nah.

                         BEN
          What you been up to?

                                             (CONTINUED)

CONTINUED: 89

                          WENDY
             Nothing.

EXT. STREET. DAY.   90

Mikey rides slowly home. At a lonely bend in the road, he
wobbles again on his bike and falls off.

                          MIKEY
             Jeez.

He stands and dusts himself off, humiliated, alone.

Motionless, rooted to the spot, a wave of awful sentiment and
fear overcomes him. He shudders at the barely audible sensation
of the now-familiar hum.

INT. HOOD LIVING ROOM. DAY.   91

Wendy enters the house and climbs the stairs.

She sees the crumpled bed sheets in her parents' room and hears
Elena in the shower.

EXT. NEW CANAAN STATION. DAY.   92

Paul walks to the parking lot with his father, who carries his
duffel bag.

EXT. STREETS. DAY.   93

Ben's car heading back to the house with Paul.

INT. HOOD CAR. DAY.   94

                       BEN
             So how's school treating you?

                       PAUL
             All right.

                       BEN
             Classes?

                       PAUL
             Good.

                                              (CONTINUED)

CONTINUED: 94

> BEN
> Grades?

> PAUL
> Fine.

> BEN
> Anyone special? You know...

> PAUL
> Hnnn.

> BEN
> Well it's good to see you -- we
> miss you around the house and all,
> but this St. Peter's, it's top of
> the line, eh?

> PAUL
> Yeah.

> BEN
> You know Paul, I've been thinking,
> maybe this is as good a time as
> any to have a little talk, you
> know, about -- well --

He makes a sharp turn. Paul puts his arms up on the dashboard
to steady himself.

> PAUL
> (nervous)
> About?

> BEN
> Well, the whole gamut. Facts of
> life and all. Some fatherly
> advice, because, I tell you,
> there's things happening that
> you're probably old enough
> to...digest.

> PAUL
> Uh...things?

Ben hesitates.

> BEN (Cont'd)
> Well... things that happen between
> a...
> (pause)
> (more)

(CONTINUED)

>   BEN (Cont'd)
>   For example, on the self-abuse
>   front -- and this is important --
>   it's not advisable to do it in the
>   shower -- it wastes water and
>   electricity and because we all
>   expect you to be doing it there in
>   any case -- and, um, not onto the
>   linen, and not on your sister's
>   underwear or any clothing
>   belonging to your mother --

He pauses to gauge the effect of his monologue on his son, then
continues.

>   PAUL
>   Uh, Dad --

Just then Ben runs a stop sign and almost slams into another
car.

>   BEN
>   Holy! Well. If you're worried
>   about anything, just feel free to
>   ask, and, uh, we can look it up.

>   PAUL
>   Uh, Dad, you know I'm 16.

>   BEN
>   All the more reason for this
>   little heart-to-heart...great.

They drive up to the house.

>   BEN
>   Um, Paul?...On second thought...

EXT. HOOD HOUSE. DAY.   95

The car pulls up and parks.

>   BEN
>   I was thinking, can you do me a
>   favor and pretend I never said any
>   of that.

>   PAUL
>   Sure, Dad.

                              (CONTINUED)

CONTINUED: 95

                         BEN
              Thanks.

Paul gets out, looking shell-shocked. He sees Wendy waving to
him from a second floor window. He nods back.

In the doorway, Elena waits.

INT. HOOD HALLWAY. DAY.   96

Paul knocks on Wendy's bedroom door. She opens it.

                         PAUL
              Hello, Charles.

                         WENDY
              Greetings, Charles.

INT. WENDY'S ROOM. DAY.   97

Paul and Wendy sit on the floor.

                         PAUL
              How are the parental units
              functioning these days?

                         WENDY
              Dad's like doing his Up With
              People routine, Mom hasn't been
              saying much.

                         PAUL
              I don't know. Dad seems a little
              weird. You know, nervous.

                         WENDY
              Yeah, well, wait till Mom finally
              opens her mouth.

They both ponder silently. Then:

                         PAUL
              You think they're headed for,
              like, the dustbin of history?

                         WENDY
              Huh?

                         PAUL
              Divorce court?

                              (CONTINUED)

CONTINUED:

                    WENDY
        They dropped out of their couples
        group therapy thing.

                    PAUL
        Is that good or bad?

She just shrugs. Silence. Then:

                    PAUL
        May I operate the telephonic
        apparatus?

                    WENDY
        Why don't you use the phone
        downstairs?

                    PAUL
        Calling an individual, Charles, in
        New York. Confirming a social
        outing for Friday night.

                    WENDY
        Can I come?

                    PAUL
        It's a one-on-one kind of date
        thing.

                    WENDY
        With who?

                    PAUL
        Her name's Libbets.

                    WENDY
        Libbets? What kind of a name is
        Libbets?

The record they've been listening begins to skip.

                    PAUL
        Hey, is that my record?

                    WENDY
        It skipped from before I borrowed
        it.

Paul goes and takes the record off the stereo.

                 (CONTINUED)

CONTINUED: (2)   97

                    PAUL
          You have messed with my shit,
          Charles.

He looks at her and shrugs -- he doesn't really mind.

EXT. HOOD HOUSE. DAY.   98

Morning. To establish.

INT. HOOD BEDROOM. DAY.   99

Elena is coming out of the master bathroom in a robe, a towel
wrapped around her head.

                    ELENA
          The turkey in?

                    BEN
          Stuffed and roasting.

INT. HOOD HALLWAY. DAY.   100

Ben Hood pads down the hall in his bathrobe, tries the bathroom
door. It's locked.

                    BEN
          Anyone home?

INT. HOOD BATHROOM. DAY.   101

The shower is running, but Paul is standing by the open window,
puffing on a joint and trying to blow the smoke outside.

                    PAUL
          I'll be out in a second.

Ben walks back to the bedroom, smirking.

                    BEN
          Sure you will.

INT. PAUL'S ROOM. DAY.   102

Paul is standing on the bed, taking his old sports posters down
from the wall.

                              (CONTINUED)

CONTINUED: 102

Elena comes to the door.

                    ELENA
          Supper's almost ready...Maybe you
          want to save those?

                    PAUL
          They've been up for too long.

                    ELENA
          You've lost your interest in
          sports?

                    PAUL
          No...just, you know, professional
          sports, opium for the masses kind
          of thing, though I'm into
          intramural, you know, less
          competitive, participation --

                    ELENA
               (smiling)
          I see.

                    PAUL
          You know, like frisbee.

Even Paul has to laugh at himself. Elena joins him.

A beat.

                    PAUL
          Um, Mom, you know Wendy was
          saying, that you and Dad...

                    ELENA
          Wendy said what?

                    PAUL
          Something about therapy?

                    ELENA
          Oh that. Well, your father and I
          thought it might help...with our
          communicating? And I think it
          did.

                    PAUL
          So you and Dad are...
          communicating?

Elena smiles reassuringly.

                                        (CONTINUED)

CONTINUED: (2)   102

                    ELENA
        Sure.

As she leaves he room, her smile fades.

INT. HOOD DINING ROOM. DAY.   103

One by one, each member of the Hood family carries in a final
item to place on the overstuffed Thanksgiving table. Then, one
by one, they each silently take their seats.

They look over the table. No one moves.

                    BEN
            Well, it's great we can all be
            together. And this Thanksgiving,
            no hysteria, no yelling,
            especially with grandpa not here,
            although we miss him. So let's do
            it right and actually, Wendy, why
            don't you say grace. You used to
            love to say grace, remember?

Wendy grimaces, as they all bow their heads slightly.

                    WENDY
            Dear Lord, thank you for this
            Thanksgiving holiday, and for all
            the material possessions that we
            have and enjoy, and for letting us
            white people kill all the
            Indians...

Everyone looks up.

                    WENDY
            ... and steal their tribal lands
            and stuff ourselves like pigs ...

Mutterings and groans: "Wendy!" "For Christ's sake" etc.

                    WENDY
            ... while children in Africa and
            Asia are napalmed and --

                    BEN
            Jesus! All right, enough! Paul
            -- gravy?

                                        (CONTINUED)

CONTINUED: 103

They all unceremoniously start to dig in.

                              FADE OUT:

EXT. CARVER HOUSE. DAY.   104

To establish.

INT. CARVER GUEST ROOM / LIVING ROOM. DAY.   105

Janey Carver is pouring Benjamin Hood a drink from a bottle of
vodka. Benjamin is already unbuttoned and shoeless; Janey still
fully dressed.

                    JANEY
          Here.

                    BEN
          After the Thanksgiving I had, I
          need it. You having one?

                    JANEY
          In a bit.

She sits next to him, he kisses the back of her neck.

                    BEN
          You know, I think Elena might
          suspect something.

Janey gives him a rather contemptuous look.

                    BEN
               (thinking aloud)
          Maybe it's all for the better, you
          know? Yesterday, at dinner, well,
          she hasn't said anything...has she
          acted funny to you, I mean, have
          you noticed anything?

                    JANEY
               (almost ironic)
          Have I noticed anything? I'm not
          married to her Benjamin, you are.
          I think you've probably a better
          vantage point from which to
          observe her.

                              (CONTINUED)

CONTINUED: 105

                         BEN
              Yeah, but, I -- I've been working
              a lot lately, and -- No, that's
              not it. I guess we've just been
              on the verge of saying something,
              whatever it is, just saying
              something to each other. On the
              verge.

Janey gets up.

                         JANEY
              I'll be back.

Benjamin looks at her quizzically.

                         BEN
              Huh?

                         JANEY
              Birth control.

                         BEN
              Right. Gotcha.

She leaves the room.

He leans back onto the bed. Sits back up. Takes a sip of
vodka. Puts the glass down. Takes his socks off. He's now in
just his jockey shorts and shirt.

Faintly, he hears a door close. The front door?

He takes another sip.

He hears another sound.

                         BEN
              Janey?

Nothing.

He goes to the door and carefully opens it.

                         BEN
                    (quietly)
              Janey?

He hears, quite audibly, a car door open, close, Janey's car
start and pull out.

                         (CONTINUED)

CONTINUED: (2)   105

He runs to a front window just in time to catch a glimpse of her
driving off.

                    BEN
          Shit.

INT. CARVER GUEST ROOM. LATER.   106

Benjamin sits on the guest bed, still in his underwear, drinking
from the bottle.

He gets up and starts to wander around the house, still holding
the bottle.

INT. CARVER MASTER BEDROOM. CONT'D.   107

Benjamin saunters through. He presses on the king-sized bed --
it undulates.

                    BEN
          Water bed! Dig it!

He wiggles comically, making more waves.

                                        JUMP CUT:

Ben idly goes through Janey's drawers.

INT. CARVER MASTER BATHROOM. CONT'D.   108

He rifles through the bathroom cabinet, checking out the
medicines.

INT. CARVER BEDROOM. CONT'D.   109

He notices a garter belt hanging from the walk-in closet door.
He picks it up and twirls it.

INT. MIKEY'S ROOM. CONT'D.   110

Benjamin walks in, an obvious look of distaste.

He sorts through a few of Mike's things -- monster eyes that
glow in the dark, The Sensuous Woman, etc.

He lifts a soiled rag from under Mikey's pillow.

                                        (CONTINUED)

CONTINUED: 110

                    BEN
          Yuck!

He puts it back.

He twirls the garter belt absent-mindedly, but then, thinking he
hears something downstairs, he freezes. Listening hard -- no
further sounds. He tosses the garter belt into the back of
Mike's closet, then cautiously walks out of the room.

INT. CARVER GUEST ROOM. CONT'D.   111

He finishes putting his clothes back on. As he reaches for the
door, he hears voices and quickly steps back in again.

Teenage voices. Mikey and Wendy.

                    MIKEY
                  (o.s.)
          See, no one's here. Maybe you
          want to go to the basement?

                    WENDY
                  (o.s.)
          Maybe we can just watch some TV.

                    MIKEY
                  (o.s.)
          There's a TV in the basement.

Hood hears their steps down into the basement.

INT. CARVER BASEMENT. DAY.   112

Wendy and Mikey stand in the middle of the semi-lit basement.

                    MIKEY
          Maybe we can mess around. You
          know, only if you want to...

                    WENDY
          I don't know.

                    MIKEY
          Why did you -- with Sandy?

                    WENDY
          I don't know.

                                        (CONTINUED)

CONTINUED: 112

                         MIKEY
               You like him? He worships you.

But Wendy doesn't seem to hear -- she's drawn to an object lying
next to a bean bag chair off to one side.

                         WENDY
               Hey, what's this?

With a look of utter fascination, she picks up a Nixon mask,
looking at it as though it were an archeological find.

                         WENDY
          Wow!

                         MIKEY
          Wendy!

She puts the mask on.

                         WENDY
                    (from behind the mask)
               I won't take my pants off. But
               I'll touch it. That's as far as
               it goes.

Mikey looks totally confused.

Remaining fully clothed, Wendy loosens Mike's belt, showing no
excitement from behind her mask, and lets him climb on top of
her for a dry hump.

Just then, a shaft of light hits them from the top of the stairs
-- Ben towers above them, looking down.

Mikey flips over immediately and pulls his clothes together,
grabbing a *TV Guide* as Wendy stands up, the mask still on.

As Ben descends, Mikey, still stuffing his shirt-tail into his
pants, pretends to flip through the *TV Guide*.

                         MIKEY
                    (muttering)
               When worlds collide.

                         WENDY
          Huh?

                         MIKEY
               4:30 movie. *When Worlds Collide.*

Ben arrives, folds his arms.

                                             (CONTINUED)

CONTINUED: (2)   112

                    BEN
          What the hell are you kids doing
          down here?

                    WENDY
          What do you think we're doing,
          Dad?

                    BEN
          What do I think? I think you're
          probably touching each other. I
          think you're touching that
          reckless jerk-off, for God's sake,
          and I think he's trying to get
          into your slacks. I think, at
          fourteen years of age, that you're
          getting ready to give up your
          girlhood --

                    MIKEY
          Hey, hang on there, Mr. Hood --

                    BEN
          Don't you direct a single word at
          me, Mikey. I don't want to hear
          it. I'll be speaking with your
          parents about this situation very
          soon. Bet your ass on that, son.
          Young lady?

                    WENDY
          Talking to me, Dad?

                    BEN
          Who else would I be talking to?
          And take that thing off!

                    WENDY
               (pulling off the mask)
          Well, then forget all this stern
          dad stuff.

                    BEN
          I'm not interested in your smart
          ass remarks now, lady. Let's go.
          Right now. You and I can discuss
          it on the walk home.

She stands next to Mikey for a moment, both on the verge of
tears.

EXT. STREET. EVENING.   113

Hood and Wendy walk through a cold drizzling rain.

He looks at her from time to time, then takes her arm.

                    BEN
          Look, kiddo, don't worry about it.
          I really don't care that much.
          I'm just not sure he's right for
          you, that's all.

                    WENDY
          Huh?

                    BEN
          It's just that you develop a sense
          when you get older, if things are
          going to work out or if they
          won't, and sometimes it's not
          worth the mess...

She looks at him. They keep walking. She walks through a
puddle.

                    BEN
          Your toes cold?

                    WENDY
          Yeah.

He stops and lifts her in his arms.

                    BEN
          I'll carry you up the drive.

She puts her arms around his neck and he lifts her up.

On her face, as he carries her -- a look of blank but real
intimacy.

INT. HOOD FRONT HALL. EVE.   114

Hood and Wendy enter, wet and cold, muttering hellos.

                    ELENA
               (o.s., from the
                kitchen)
          Dinner in ten minutes.

                    BEN
          You go dry off now.

Wendy heads for the stairs, Hood following.

INT. HOOD BEDROOM. EVE.   115

Hood finishes taking off his wet clothes as Elena enters and
turns on a light. She stands watching him.

                    BEN
          Hey, should I dress for the
          Halford's now, or -- give me
          your --

                    ELENA
          Up to you. I'd like to go early
          and leave pretty soon after that.

                    BEN
          I get you loud and clear...hey,
          you look nice.

                    ELENA
          Thanks...So where've you two been?

                    BEN
               (pause)
          You'll never guess where I found
          her.

Not much response from Elena.

                    ELENA
          You found her?

                    BEN
          In the basement over at Janey and
          Jim's. With that weirdo Mikey.
          Not even a TV on. And they're on
          the floor and he's got his
          trousers down though thank
          goodness she's still dressed.
          Well, I really let him have it!
               (a nervous laugh)
          ...and Wendy came home
          peacefully...

                    ELENA
               (pause)
          So what were you doing in the
          Carvers' basement, anyway?

                    BEN
          Oh, just dropping off a coffee
          cup. Jim left it, last time he
          was over. It was on the dash of
          the car.
               (more)

                                          (CONTINUED)

CONTINUED: 115

                         BEN (Cont'd)
              You were, you know, reading. I
              thought I'd just catch some air.

                         ELENA
              Oh right. The mustache coffee
              cup. The one that was sitting on
              the dash.

                         BEN
              Yeah, that one.

                         ELENA
              That one.

She walks down to the kitchen, Benjamin following her.

INT. HOOD KITCHEN. NIGHT.   116

A silent dinner of turkey sandwiches with Elena, Benjamin, and
Wendy. The turkey carcass sits, embarrassed, in the middle of
the table.

Paul enters.

                         PAUL
              See you.

                         BEN
              Stay out of trouble.

                         ELENA
              You'll be on the 10:30 train?

                         PAUL
              11:30?

                         ELENA
              Paul --

                         BEN
              Ah let the guy have his fun.
              What's the name of this girl with
              the Park Avenue address?

                         PAUL
              Libbets. Libbets Casey.

                         BEN
              Libbets? What kind of name is
              Libbets?

                                                         (CONTINUED)

CONTINUED: 116

>   ELENA
>   You'll get a taxi home from the
>   station tonight? It's supposed to
>   storm.

Paul shrugs and is out the door.

The meal continues.

Wendy, finished, gets up from the table. Opens the fridge, but finds nothing. Then goes to the candy shelf and grabs some Hot Tamales, leaving the room without a word and going into the den.

INT. HOOD DEN. NIGHT.   117

Wendy turns the TV on.

>   TV
>   ... and that ends today's
>   highlight coverage of the
>   Watergate affair.

>   WENDY
>   Shoot.

She changes the channel. A weather report is in progress.

>   WEATHERMAN
>   (on TV)
>   As the cold front moves in, expect
>   rapidly decreasing temperatures
>   tonight, and be careful of ice on
>   the roads as that downpour gets to
>   freezing...

INT. HOOD KITCHEN. NIGHT.   118

Ben and Elena rise from the table with their dishes.

>   BEN
>   What's for dessert?

>   ELENA
>   See for yourself.

>   BEN
>   No advice from the experts, huh?

His plate slips out of his hands into the trash. He fishes it out and sets it on the counter.

>   (CONTINUED)

CONTINUED: 118

                         ELENA
               Don't start.

                         BEN
               You think I --

                         ELENA
               I have no idea.

                         BEN
               What's on your mind? Don't --

                         ELENA
               It wouldn't make a pleasant
               evening, if that's what you're
               after. I don't want to talk about
               it. Stupid mustache cup.

                         BEN
               What do you mean?

                         ELENA
               Don't be dim.

INT. HOOD DEN. NIGHT.   119

Wendy puts the volume of the TV up, to drown out a conversation
she can almost overhear but doesn't want to.

INT. HOOD KITCHEN. NIGHT. CONT'D.   120

                         ELENA
               Oh, lord. You think I'm so dense.
               And now you want to be seen with
               your dense wife at the cocktail
               party. You want to wear that
               ridiculous shirt which doesn't go
               with those pants at all. You want
               to wear that, and you want me to
               shake hands with your friends and
               make conversation and dress up in
               an outfit that shows a lot of
               cleavage and you're not going to
               accord me the respect of talking
               honestly about this...You don't
               really know what this feels like.

                                        (CONTINUED)

CONTINUED: 120

> BEN
> (whispering)
> Sure I do. Do I know what
> loneliness feels like? Sure I do.
> I know a lot about it, if that's
> what you mean.

> ELENA
> Benjamin. That's supposed to
> explain it?

> BENJAMIN
> Explain? I didn't -- technically
> -- it's not what you're thinking
> Elena.

> ELENA
> Please have the decency to at
> least not tell me what I'm
> thinking.

Elena sighs, then walks into the den.

INT. HOOD DEN. NIGHT.   121

> ELENA
> We're going to the Halford's. The
> number's on the calendar in the
> kitchen. We should be home around
> 11.

> WENDY
> (eyes still glued to
> the TV)
> Is it a big party? A big
> neighborhood party?

> ELENA
> I suppose. Why?

> WENDY
> Just curious. If there's a
> problem, I guess I'll just call
> you there to interrupt.

> ELENA
> What sort of problems are you
> planning exactly?

Elena kisses the top of her head.

                                            (CONTINUED)

CONTINUED: 121

>   WENDY
>   (still watching the TV)
>   Oh, I thought I'd steal the
>   station wagon, drive up to a
>   commune. Or set the house on
>   fire. You know.

>   ELENA
>   Just bundle up. It's supposed to
>   freeze tonight. We'll see you in
>   the morning.

EXT. HOOD HOUSE. NIGHT.   122

Elena and Ben emerge from the house, and look up at a darkening,
foreboding sky. A light rain falls. They jog toward their car.

INT/EXT. HOOD CAR. NIGHT.   123

The car moves slowly through the rainy suburban streets.

Inside, Elena and Ben don't speak.

EXT. HALFORD HOUSE. NIGHT.   124

Their Firebird pulls up. There are already many other cars
parked on the lawn and driveway.

INT. HALFORD FOYER. NIGHT.   125

Ben and Elena enter. Dot Halford accosts them.

>   DOT
>   Ben, Elena. Wonderful!
>   Wonderful! So wonderful to see
>   you.

Finishing the last of a celery canoe, she kisses the air next to
Ben's ear and gives Elena a manic hug.

Then, picking up a white salad bowl from the hall table:

>   DOT
>   Would you care to play? New this
>   year.

Close on: the bowl full of keys.

                                                    (CONTINUED)

CONTINUED: 125

              DOT
      Strictly volunteer, of course.
      You can put your coats in the
      library if you like.

             ELENA
      Oh, damn. Uh, I've left the --

             BEN
      You've...

             ELENA
      In the car.

             BEN
      Oh, yeah. Yeah, we'll be right
      back, Dot.

INT/EXT. HOOD CAR. CONT'D.   126

Ben and Elena climb back in the car and close the doors,
shivering.

             ELENA
      This just isn't the best moment
      for this.

             BEN
      I know, I know. I had no idea --

             ELENA
      That this was going to be a key
      party?

             BEN
      Yeah, well, if we'd understood we
      could have invented some kind of
      excuse. A key party -- did you
      see how stuffed that bowl was
      already?

             ELENA
      Well?

             BEN
      I think we're here and we don't
      have to stay -- we ought simply to
      put in an appearance and then we
      can head home.

                    (CONTINUED)

                        ELENA
              Damn it, Ben --

                        BEN
              I'm not staying at this party so
              we can go home with someone else's
              wife. That's not why we're here,
              right? We're simply being
              neighbors here, and I think we
              should do just that --

                        ELENA
              You're not going to --

                        BEN
              I'm not.

                        ELENA
              You have some marker, that's what
              I think, if you want to know the
              truth. You have some marker and
              you're going to put it on the
              house keys so that Janey can find
              them and then when I get back to
              the house I'll find the two of you
              in there and Wendy'll be able to
              hear you and Paul will be back and
              he'll hear you and I'll catch you,
              that's what I think. She'll be
              swearing and banging against the
              wall and I'll catch --

                        BEN
              Elena.

She rubs her eyes.

                        BEN
              Elena, it's not what you think.
              It's not a big plot. Honestly.
              Honestly. I don't know if you
              want to go over this now, but it's
              just something that comes over me.
              I don't feel good about it. I
              know I've done what I didn't want
              to do. I don't know --

                        ELENA
              Well, I'm really pleased to hear a
              confession.

                                        (CONTINUED)

CONTINUED: (2)   126

                    BEN
          Elena, you're just getting wound
          up to get wound up.

                    ELENA
          Thanks for the diagnosis, Ben.
          Thank you. So let's just go to
          this fiasco if that's what you
          want to do. Let's just go on in.
          I'd rather talk to anyone else but
          you.

She pulls the keys out of the ignition, gets out of the car, and
slams the door. He follows her.

INT. HALFORD FOYER. NIGHT.   127
                    ELENA
          Oh, Dot!

Elena, entering the house again, tosses the keys at Dot Halford,
who looks surprised.

Ben slides in behind his wife.

Dot drops the keys into the bowl.

Slow-motion, close up: the keys, on their equine chain, fall in
with a THUNDEROUS CRASH.

INT. HALFORD LIVING ROOM. CONT'D.   128

The room is crowded with nervous, expectant couples and various
groupings.

Elena slips into a side room.

Benjamin heads over immediately to the drink table and pours a
stiff one, turning around to find at his elbow none other than
George Clair.

                    GEORGE
          Benjie!

                    BEN
          Clair, George Clair! What the
          hell brings you to New Canaan?

                              (CONTINUED)

CONTINUED:

                    GEORGE
Well, it's the funniest thing.
I've been talking to some
investors -- a little outside
venture, you understand, between
you and me -- about a scheme to
manufacture a new Styrofoam
packaging. Little peanut-like
pieces that can really keep an
item free from trauma during
shipping. Miraculous. Anyway, it
turns out the genius behind the
whole project is your neighbor,
Jim Carver. How about that!

                    BEN
Well, hey, isn't that a one-in-a-
million coincidence. A real
dreamer, Jim Carver, eh?

                    GEORGE
Darned right. Look here, Benj,
whaddya make of this sequel to *The
Godfather?* You think it's gonna
work?

                    BEN
Don't see how. I think the
public's had its fill of this
gangster stuff. No, trust me --
disaster pics. And air hockey.

                    GEORGE
Yeah, good.

Benjamin catches a glimpse of Janey, voluptuously attired,
across the room.

                    GEORGE
Well, gonna make a break for the
hors d'oeuvres guy.

                    BEN
Yeah, see you bright and early
Monday A.M.
      (beat)
Say, where's the wife?

                    GEORGE
    (winking as he goes)
In Rhode Island with the folks.
I'm a free agent tonight.

                          (CONTINUED)

At this, they both notice Elena slowly gliding across the other side of the room. Clair gives Ben a sideways glance, then moves on.

Ben makes straight for Janey, who pretends to be preoccupied with a plant.

                    JANEY
          Oh jeez, Benjie. Well, here you
          are.

                    BEN
          Damn right, but where the hell
          were you?

                    JANEY
              (looking around)
          What are you talking about?

                    BEN
              (whispering, but too
               loudly)
          Don't bullshit me around, Janey.
          Jesus Christ, I waited around for
          more than half an hour, in nothing
          but my boxer shorts, and -- and
          what's all that about? What the
          hell happened?

Janey takes a sip of her drink.

                    JANEY
          A prior engagement overcame me.

                    BEN
          What?

                    JANEY
          Listen, Benjamin Hood. I have
          obligations that precede your. . .
          from before you showed up. One or
          two, you know, good-natured
          encounters, that doesn't mean I'm
          . . . I'm not just some toy for
          you. When I remembered some
          chores I wanted to get done before
          the party, I just did them, that's
          all, because I wanted to do them
          before I saw Jimmy.

                              (CONTINUED)

CONTINUED: (3)   128

                    BEN
          Jimmy? Jimmy? I don't know how
          to take this. And what do you
          mean, Jimmy? I thought you said
          you and your husband --

                    JANEY
          How you take it isn't all that
          interesting to me, Benjamin. I'm
          sorry --

                    BEN
          I just can't believe you could be
          so --

Stalling, he watches her take another sip of her drink and
wander off.

The air is filled with talk of Watergate, Billie Jean King, the
Oil Crisis, the Mets.

Benjamin goes over to the couch, where Dave Gorman is chatting
up an attractive younger woman.

                    GORMAN
               (lighting up a joint)
          Welcome to the Monkey House has
          been a seminal influence on me --
          hey Benjamin -- give it a try?
          This stuff will make some sense
          out of those larger questions.

                    BEN
               (waving it away)
          Thanks for the advice Dave.

But then, Benjamin changes his mind.

                    BEN
          Uh, well, what the hey...

Taking he joint, he tugs on it, holding the smoke in his lungs.

                    BEN
               (coughing)
          Good shit.

                    GORMAN
          Sure is good shit. It's opiated.
          I had it in my chamber for a
          while. I was smoking this
          other --

                                              (CONTINUED)

CONTINUED: (4)   128

                    BEN
          It's what?

                    GORMAN
          Don't fret, Benjie, it's --

                    BEN
          Darn it, Dave.

He rises unsteadily, weaving through the room's conversations.

                    JACK MOELLERING
          Take California. They've got
          their own airline in-state that's
          not subject to the fare controls.
          Compare Sacramento to LA on the
          controlled airlines and you'll see
          what Friedman is saying -- supply
          and demand, less restriction.

Benjamin walks over to a window. The outdoor lamps illuminate a
new and heavy downpour of frozen sleet.

INT. CONRAIL TRAIN. NIGHT.   129

Paul is seated, reading the latest number of *The Fantastic Four*
comic book. The cover displays a lurid, atomically glowing
baby.

The conductor walks through the cabin.

                    CONDUCTOR
          Approaching our final stop, Grand
          Central Station.

Paul looks out the window at the tenements of Harlem, barely
visible through the walls of sleet. Soon the train enters the
tunnel toward the station.

EXT. PARK AVENUE APARTMENT BUILDING. NIGHT.   130

Paul gets out of a cab and heads inside. He's met by the
doorman.

                    PAUL
          Libbets Casey, please.

                    DOORMAN
          Your name?

                                        (CONTINUED)

CONTINUED: 130

                         PAUL
               Paul Hood.

                         DOORMAN
                    (a smirk)
               Elevator on the right. Eighth
               floor -- she's waiting for you.

INT. HALL IN FRONT OF LIBBETS' DOOR. NIGHT.   131

Paul rings the bell.

                         LIBBETS
                    (o.s., from the other
                     side of the door)
               Open it, Paul!

Paul opens the door, and enters the apartment.

INT. LIBBETS' APARTMENT. NIGHT.   13

It's half dark, has an air of old wealth.

Libbets skids across the parquet floor to him.

                         LIBBETS
               Excellent. We were waiting!

She turns and runs into the den.

                         PAUL
                    (under his breath)
               We?

And there, in the den, cleaning an ounce of dope on an open copy
of Nixon's *Six Crises,* is -- Francis.

                         FRANCIS
                    (lifting the book up)
               You oughtta read this Hood, Nixon,
               our leader, all ye need know about
               the travails of life. Check out
               the Checkers speech stuff.

                         PAUL
                    (all hope drained from
                     him)
               Francis. You gonna leave the
               seeds in there? In the binding
               like that?

                                                          (CONTINUED)

>   FRANCIS
>   All will be revealed, baby.

The television is turned on to a weather report about the ice
storm.

>   FRANCIS
>   Awesome sleet and rain.

>   LIBBETS
>   Major.

>   FRANCIS
>   Hey there. You, young knight.
>   Can you check on the mead? Can
>   you sally forth and secure us some
>   more mead?

>   PAUL
>   Huh?

>   FRANCIS
>   (nasal voice,
>   impersonating a TV
>   character)
>   Moisture! Moisture!

>   LIBBETS
>   (pointing)
>   Beer. In the pantry.

Paul trudges disconsolately out of the room.

INT. LIBBETS' KITCHEN. NIGHT   133

Paul, after wandering a maze of halls, enters the kitchen, where
he takes a six-pack out of the fridge and returns to the living
room.

INT. LIBBETS' LIVING ROOM. NIGHT   134

He enters the room with the beer.

>   LIBBETS
>   Frankie opens them with his teeth.

>   PAUL
>   (handing him a beer)
>   Hey, it's a sellable skill.

                              (CONTINUED)

84.

CONTINUED: 134

Francis licks closed a second joint, then takes the beer and
opens it with his rear molars.

FRANCIS
          Hell on the fillings.

Paul opens the other two beers and hands one to Libbets. They
light up a joint.

FRANCIS
          Everything's gonna freeze, the big
          freeze.

LIBBETS
          Yeah, Paul, are you gonna get home
          okay?

Paul and Francis exchange a look.

She puts an Allman Brothers tape on the 8-track and turns the TV
down.

INT. HOOD HOUSE. NIGHT.   135

Wendy wanders desultorily through the house. She walks into her
parents' bedroom and lies down on the bed. She sticks her legs
up into the air for a few seconds, then lets them down. She
gets back up and walks into the hall.

INT. HOOD BATHROOM. NIGHT.   136

Wendy enters the bathroom.

She fills the sink with water, then turns off the tap. She
takes a razor blade from the counter, and slowly, determinedly,
holds it to her wrist.

She presses it into her skin, drawing a small drop of blood.

WENDY
          Ouch!

She drops the blade and splashes water on her wrist, grabbing
some toilet paper and holding it against the tiny wound.

WENDY
          Stupid.

She hears the phone ring and walks downstairs.

                    SANDY
          Where you going?

                    MIKEY
          Out.

                    SANDY
          It's freezing.

                    MIKEY
               (pausing)
          Yeah.

                    SANDY
          Then why you going out?

                    MIKEY
               (thinking)
          When it freezes, I guess that
          means the molecules are not
          moving. So when you breathe,
          there's nothing in the air, you
          know, to breathe in to your body.
          The molecules have stopped. It's
          clean.

just looks at him. He walks out into the night.

IALFORD HOUSE. NIGHT.   140

sits on a couch, talking to no one, barely looking up,
someone stands in front of her.

                    ELENA
          Reverend Edwards.

                    PHILIP
          Perhaps you might find it in your
          heart to call me Philip?

:s beside her.

                    ELENA
          You're here...I'm a bit surprised.

                    PHILIP
          Sometimes the shepherd needs the
          company of the sheep.

                              (CONTINUED)

INT. HOOD DEN. NIGHT.

Wendy picks up the phone.

                    WENDY
          Hood residence.

INT. CARVER KITCHEN. NIGHT.

Mikey is on the other end of the line.

                    MIKEY
          Your parents at that party?

                    WENDY
          Yeah. Yours?

                    MIKEY
          You get in trouble?

                    WENDY
          Maybe. Can't really tell yet.

                    MIKEY
          I'm sorry if I got you into
          trouble. Maybe we don't have to,
          you know...unless you really want
          to.

                    WENDY
          Yeah.

                    MIKE
          I'm going to Silver Meadow, check
          out the ice storm...You wanna
          come?

                    WENDY
          Maybe. I don't know.

                    MIKE
          Yeah. OK. If you're there, I'll
          look for you.

INT. CARVER HOUSE. NIGHT.

Mikey, bundled up in a huge orange ski parka an
the door.

Sandy is watching Time Tunnel on the TV.

                              (CONTI

CONTINUED: 140

> ELENA
> I'm going to try hard <u>not</u> to
> understand the implications of
> that simile.

Philip's about to reply, but thinks better of it.

They sit glumly next to each other for a minute. Then Philip
rises.

> PHILIP
> Forgive me.

> ELENA
> Philip?

He walks swiftly to the hall and hurriedly fishes his keys out
of the bowl, then heads for the door. Elena has gotten up to
follow him.

> TED FRANKLIN
> (passing by)
> I hope those weren't <u>my</u> keys.

He laughs at his own joke as Philip rushes out the front door.
Elena watches him go, even more forlorn than before.

INT. LIBBETS' BATHROOM. NIGHT.   141

Paul enters the bathroom. We hear Francis' and Libbets' voices
from the other room, laughing.

He pees.

At the sink, he pauses in front of the medicine cabinet, then
opens it.

> PAUL
> Eureka.

He pulls out some bottles.

> PAUL
> Valium. Seconal. Uh,
> (can't quite pronounce
> this one)
> Par-er-goric?
> (more)

                                            (CONTINUED)

CONTINUED: 141

>   PAUL (Cont'd)
>   (a beat, looking into
>   the mirror for effect
>   while holding up the
>   Seconal)
>   Francis Davenport the Fourth --
>   tonight you sleep the sleep of the
>   just.

He pockets the Seconal and turns out the light.

INT. LIBBETS' DEN. NIGHT.   142

Paul re-enters the den to find Francis alone.

>   PAUL
>   And whence has yon virginal maiden
>   absconded?

>   FRANCIS
>   Like into one of the other 20 or
>   so bathrooms they've got in this
>   place.

Paul takes out the bottle and opens it.

>   PAUL
>   Check it out. Not for the faint
>   of heart.

>   FRANCIS
>   Pharmaceutical! You are a god.

>   PAUL
>   (picking up beer,
>   trying to hurry before
>   Libbets returns)
>   One for you and one for me.

He hands a pill to Francis, then pretends to pop one into his
mouth and takes a swig of his beer. As Francis downs his own,
Paul pockets his unswallowed pill.

>   LIBBETS
>   (in the doorway)
>   No candy for me?

>   (CONTINUED)

CONTINUED: 142

                        FRANCIS
            Groovy.
                (to Paul)
            Young master of the revels, a
            treat for our hostess?

                        PAUL
            Well, uh, I don't, it's really --

                        LIBBETS
            What is it?

                        FRANCIS
            Come on Paulie, share the wealth.
            You copped 'em from her mom's
            stash anyway.

                        LIBBETS
            Let's see!

                        PAUL
                (hand in pocket)
            Libbets, you really shouldn't mix
            and match, you know with the beer.
            I'll put 'em back.

Libbets reaches into his pocket and pulls out the bottle.

                        LIBBETS
            Oh far out, Paulie. Hey look,
            these expired like five months
            ago. You think they're better
            aged?

She opens up the bottle and takes one out.

                        PAUL
            Maybe you should have just a half.

                        LIBBETS
            Thanks for the advice, Dad.

She takes the pill.

Paul looks on, thwarted.

INT. HALFORD HOUSE. NIGHT.   143

Ben is back at the bar, pouring another tall one. Mark Boland
sidles up next to him.

                                    (CONTINUED)

CONTINUED: 143

                    BOLAND
        Benjie, feeling no pain.

                    BEN
        As the Indian saying goes, pain is
        merely an opinion.

                    BOLAND
          (nodding across the
          room)
        Hey -- check it out. Maria
        Conrad's brought her son.
          (walking off)
        I wish some of the gang had
        brought their daughters!

Ben feels a wave of distaste at the joke.

He looks across the room as Maria and her son Neil (18, stringy
hair, acne, tie-dyed turtleneck, patched jeans) are engaging
Janey in conversation.

INT. LIBBETS' LIVING ROOM. NIGHT.   144

Paul, Francis, and Libbets sit on the floor, listening to the
music blasting at full strength.

Libbets and Francis are obviously on the verge of
unconsciousness. Paul regards them with a look of apprehension
on his face.

INT. HALFORD HOUSE. NIGHT.   145

Neil has now cornered Janey.

                    NEIL
        As Werner says, there is nothing
        to get. That's *It*. When you get
        that there's nothing to get.
        That's the training, when you ask
        yourself, the question, "What is
        is?"

                    JANEY
        Wait, this is the training, where
        they don't let you go to the
        bathroom?

                         (CONTINUED)

CONTINUED: 145

                    NEIL
          That was the hardest part. But I
          did it. And you get into some
          far-out shit.

INT. LIBBETS' LIVING ROOM. NIGHT.   146

Libbets puts a blanket over a sleeping Francis, who's crashed
out on the floor in a corner. Francis alternates between snores
and various mumbled delirious ravings.

                    FRANCIS
          The foot...the foot...toe clipper
          man...

Paul is sitting on the couch, and Libbets comes back and sits at
his feet, facing up to him.

                    PAUL
          I guess he's just real exhausted
          from, you know, tests and stuff.

Libbets is herself somewhat in dreamland.

                    LIBBETS
          Yeah.

                    PAUL
          You know Libbets, I really feel,
          you know, like a real connection
          to you --

                    LIBBETS
          Yeah but you don't even know me
          really.

                    PAUL
          Sure I do, you know, like your
          aura. That you give off.

                    LIBBETS
          My what?

                    PAUL
          It's like very positive, and I
          feel a real special feeling,
          because you really --

                    LIBBETS
          And I have a special feeling too,
          because I do. It's special.

                              (CONTINUED)

CONTINUED: 146

                              PAUL
                    You do? I'm glad. Because I feel
                    for you --

                              LIBBETS
                    And I have a feeling for you too,
                    because to me you're just like a--
                    I feel for you like you're my own
                    -- you're just like a--

                              PAUL AND LIBBETS
                              (simultaneously)
                    -- a brother.

                              PAUL
                    Yeah, you're not alone with that
                    line.

                              LIBBETS
                    I do. You are.

                              PAUL
                    Right. Cool. So, how about we
                    take a bath together?

                              LIBBETS
                              (consciousness fading
                               fast)
                    Hah, hah, you're funny. A bath.
                    Like a brother and sister. Oh
                    man, I'm so wasted.

Her head bobs and weaves, her eyes close, and suddenly her head
falls forward with a whoosh toward the couch -- smack dab
between Paul's legs.

She begins to snore instantly, her open mouth nuzzling into his
crotch.

Paul doesn't move, doesn't even breathe. Then, slowly, he leans
his back into the couch, without shifting the rest of his body.

He looks as though he has simultaneously won the lottery and
received a lobotomy.

INT. HALFORD HOUSE. NIGHT.   147

The crowd's a bit thinner than before.

As Dot Halford begins calling out for everyone's attention, a
few couples make their embarrassed, last-minute way to the door.

                              (CONTINUED)

CONTINUED: 147

> DOT
> OK everyone. We have a little
> business to attend to now. So
> everyone who'd like to stay,
> please gather in the living room.

She scoops up the bowl and places it on a high end table which
has been put in the middle of the room.

There's an air of abject nervousness, as some couples leave,
some fake-happily put their arms around each other, and still
others circle, alone, slightly perspiring.

> BEN
> (walking up to Elena)
> Ready to go?

> ELENA
> We're not going anywhere.

Elena waves at Janey Carver, who is standing across the living
room.

Janey looks back, without expression.

INT. LIBBETS' APARTMENT. NIGHT.   148

Libbets and Paul in the same position whence last we saw them.

Paul delicately leans to one side of the couch and picks up a
phone. He dials a number.

                              INTERCUT:

INT. HOOD LIVING ROOM. NIGHT.   149

The phone rings. Wendy picks it up.

> WENDY
> Hood residence.

> PAUL
> (whispering)
> Charles?

> WENDY
> Charles?

> PAUL
> It is I.

                                        (CONTINUED)

94.

CONTINUED: 149

                         WENDY
               Isn't it like time for your train?

                         PAUL
               That's, um, why I was calling.
               I'm, uh, in the midst of a moral
               dilemma. And I was wondering,
               because I know you're a very moral
               person, and --

                         WENDY
               And?

Libbets moans and pushes her open mouth even further into his
lap.

                         PAUL
               Shit, Charles. I can't really
               talk about it right now. I guess
               I better get to the train.

                         WENDY
               Whatever.

Paul hangs up the phone and looks down at Libbets.

Libbets' Allman Brothers tape has run out. The machine makes a
repeated clicking sound as the take up reel continues to circle.
The only other sound is the noise of the wind and rain lashing
against the apartment's windows.

EXT. HOOD HOUSE. NIGHT.   150

Wendy emerges from the house and gets on her bike, but the ice
makes it too slippery. The storm is now in full swing. She
gets off, lets the bike fall to the ground, and walks.

EXT. STREET. NIGHT.   151

Wendy walks, barely keeping her balance in the wind. She pauses
at the same lonely corner where Mikey had earlier stopped and
had his brief epiphany.

She shivers, feeling the same cold breath that had touched him a
few days before.

INT. HALFORD HOUSE. NIGHT.   152

All the couples are now gathered for the key selection process,
men on one side of the room, women on the other. The storm can
be heard outside.

                    DOT
               Well, what shall the order be,
               alphabetical? In order of
               appearance?

                    PIERCE SAWYER
               Golf handicap! Lowest handicap
               does the honors.

Nervous laughter.

                    DOT
               Golf handicap? Ladies, isn't it
               up to you?

                    MARIA CONRAD
               Oh I'll go first, damn it. Let's
               just line up and get it over with.

Maria chooses Stephen Earle. Hands the keys to him. A
smattering of applause as she takes his arm and they leave.

                    MARIE EARLE
               Good luck!

Neil watches his mother's exit.

                                        JUMP CUT TO:

A few more couplings.

                                        JUMP CUT TO:

Helen Worthington approaches the bowl. Helen Worthington has
the size and shape of a sumo wrestler.

There is a nervous shifting of weight on the male side of the
room.

Helen delicately reaches into the bowl. Her hands emerge with a
key chain.

George Clair steps forward, obviously depressed, as a collective
sigh of relief goes up from behind him. Ben looks on,
momentarily triumphant.

                              (CONTINUED)

Elena smiles to herself.

                              JUMP CUT TO:

The Gadds choose each other.

                    MRS. GADD
          Oh, my own husband. Isn't that
          against the rules?

                    DOT
          Try again?

                    MRS. GADD
               (relieved)
          Oh, I think not.

Mr.Gadd smiles as they leave, obviously happy to go.

Finally, only Mark Boland, Neil Conrad, Janey and Jim Carver,
Rob and Dot Halford, Sari Steele, Benjamin and Elena.

                    DOT
          Getting down to the wire!

Janey steps forward. Benjamin is obviously agitated.

Close on Janey's hands selecting -- away from Ben's equine key
ring.

She lifts up another key ring -- Neil Conrad, the teenager.

She hands the self-important-looking Neil his keys and they turn
to go.

Jim Carver smiles mysteriously to himself.

Ben suddenly lurches forward, semi-drunkenly, trying to separate
Neil from Janey.

                    THE GROUP
               (ad lib)
          Hey, hey, Ben, hang on there a
          sec.

He backs off, ashamed, and, taking a step backwards, trips over
the coffee table.

Mark Boland helps lift him up.

                    BEN
          Sorry...maybe I should...the
          bathroom?

                              (CONTINUED)

CONTINUED: (2)   152

                        DOT
            Right down the hall, Ben.

                        BEN
                    (muttering)
            Sorry, I'm sorry. Uh, I'll be
            back.

Dot follows Mark Boland down the hall behind Ben.

Suddenly, it's just Elena and Jim Carver, and Sari Steele and
Rob Halford.

                        ROB HALFORD
                    (taking Sari's arm)
            Actually, we didn't put our keys
            in at all. But you won't spread
            it around? It's my party, and Dot
            isn't... hey, we're just going to
            slip upstairs for a while. You
            folks like a cup of coffee or
            something before we go?

Elena and Jim look at each other.

                        ELENA
            Rob, we'll fix it for ourselves.
            You two go and get acquainted.
            We'll let ourselves out the front
            door.

Jim and Elena stand there alone.

                        JIM
            Well, I have to say I don't have
            much faith that my car keys are
            still in that bowl. Doesn't seem
            entirely safe, leaving your car
            keys around?

                        ELENA
            Let me.

She takes the bowl and dips her hand in. Two sets are left.
One, her own, she avoids. She takes out Jim's keys and walks
across the room, handing them to him.

                        JIM
            Thanks, but -- oh, I don't think
            so. It's been kind of a
            discouraging evening.

                                        (CONTINUED)

CONTINUED: (3)   152

                    ELENA
          You couldn't have hoped for much
          better when you came up the walk.

                    JIM
          Somehow it was different in my
          imagination when I thought about
          it. Actually, I didn't think
          about it at all, really.

They sit down on the sofa.

                    JIM
          You want coffee or something?

                    ELENA
          Well, maybe they have one of those
          filter jobs in the kitchen --

                    JIM
          Look, Elena, the fact that we're
          neighbors...you know, close
          friends, well it sort of makes
          this a little strange, don't you
          think?

                    ELENA
          My husband is probably passed out
          in the bathroom, or at least he
          wishes he were. I've been married
          to him for 17 years and I don't
          have any intention of going in
          there to get him... So what I'm
          proposing is that since your wife
          has gone off with a boy, and since
          you are standing here alone, I'm
          proposing that you and I do what
          makes sense. Stay warm. Pass
          some time. That's all.

They both look at their hands.

                    ELENA
          Now don't make me feel as if I'm
          being too forward, OK? If you
          don't --

                    JIM
          What the hey. Let's go for a
          drive.

                              (CONTINUED)

CONTINUED: (4)   152

                         ELENA
              Okay. Shall we clean up around
              here first? Do you think it's all
              right --

                         JIM
              Nah, that wasn't in the contract.

But they still walk around turning off lights.

In the hallway, Elena looks a bit mournfully at the light
seeping from underneath the bathroom door. She hears the sound
of running water from inside.

Then she goes into a sideroom and joins Jim. They pick up their
coats.

EXT. HALFORD HOUSE. NIGHT.   153

Elena and Jim walk outside into the freezing, pelting rain.

Covering their faces, they jog to his car, an oversized
Cadillac. A thick glaze of ice forms on his windshield.

INT. JIM'S CADILLAC. NIGHT.   154

They climb in.

                         JIM
              We're going to have to defrost
              this thing for a while.

He turns on the ignition, and the vents start to blow cold air
at them.

He leans over and kisses her.

                         ELENA
              Do these seats go back?

That starts it. He jumps at her, unbuckling her and unzipping
himself.

They tangle uncomfortably for a few seconds. And then,
comically, he's in her.

With a groan, it's over in a flash.

Jim pulls himself off, readjusting his pants.

                                        (CONTINUED)

CONTINUED: 154

> JIM
> That was awful, really awful. I'm
> so sorry, Elena.

Elena has somehow worked herself into the cavity of the glove
compartment, and is trying to figure out how to extricate
herself.

> JIM
> Things are really rotten at home.
> You wouldn't believe how rotten.
> Janey's sick. She's unstable, I
> guess. . .it's not the right time
> to tell you. . .but that's it --
> it's like I can't make her happy,
> the boys can't make her happy, she
> just doesn't ---

> ELENA
> Jim, maybe we should just go.
> I've got to look in on the kids.
> Paul is supposed to be coming back
> in from the city.

> JIM
> Jesus, let me make it up to you --
> I can do better than that,
> honestly --

> ELENA
> Well, we can talk about it.

> JIM
> That's fine. I wouldn't expect
> you to see it any other way.

> ELENA
> Maybe you just need -- look, can
> you wait here a sec, I need to
> tidy up -- just a minute, I'll be
> right back. You'll wait?

> JIM
> Of course.

She opens the door and walks back to the house.

INT. HALFORD HOUSE. NIGHT. 155

Elena hesitantly walks to the bathroom.

(CONTINUED)

CONTINUED: 155

She opens the door. Ben's sitting on the floor, next to the
toilet, woozily flipping through the pages of a magazine.

                    BEN
          Elena.

                    ELENA
          Ben, I've got a ride home. Maybe
          you should sleep this one off on
          the couch here?

                    BEN
          I'll drive you --

                    ELENA
          Ben.

She sits on the toilet next to him, stroking his hair.

                    ELENA
          You're in no condition to drive.
          We'll talk in the morning, OK?

He sits, accepting and quiet.

                    ELENA
          You'll get some sleep on the couch
          out there?

                    BEN
               (looking up at her,
                with gratitude)
          Sure. I'll try. And we'll talk
          in the morning?

                    ELENA
          We'll talk in the morning.

EXT. CARVER HOUSE. NIGHT.   156

Wendy walks up the drive in the rain, pauses, then goes to the
front door and knocks lightly. The door swings ajar. She
pushes on it, and lets herself in.

INT. CARVER HOUSE. NIGHT.   157

                    WENDY
          Anyone home? Hello.

                              (CONTINUED)

Wendy wanders into the living room, then climbs the steps. The
sound of the wind and the darkness begin to scare her.

She goes into Mikey's room -- it's even more of a disaster zone
than usual.

She sees on the wall his dark-light poster of the 12 (sexual)
positions of the zodiac.

She notices the black garter belt on the floor, and picks it up,
absent-mindedly swinging it in her hand as she walks out of the
room.

She walks back down the stairs and into the kitchen, leaving the
garter belt on the counter.

She opens the refrigerator, grabs a jar of peanut butter, and
scoops some up in her finger. As she puts her finger in her
mouth --

                    SANDY
          Wendy.

She gives out a little yelp.

                    WENDY
          Sandy, you scared the shit out of
          me.

                    SANDY
          What are you doing?

                    WENDY
          Just thought I'd stop by.

                    SANDY
          Mike's out -- I think he went to
          Silver Meadow to see if you were
          hanging around there.

                    WENDY
          Yeah.

                    SANDY
               (pause)
          Are you his girlfriend?

                    WENDY
          No.

INT. JIM'S CADILLAC. NIGHT.   158

Elena gets in. They drive off silently.

EXT. STREETS. NIGHT.   159

The car moves haltingly through the sleet and ice, inches up a
hill, then falters and slides back silently, circling a couple
of times before crashing into an embankment.

INT. JIM'S CADILLAC. NIGHT.   160

As the car slides and crashes amid Jim's and Elena's screams.

Silence.

                    JIM
          You okay?

                    ELENA
          Yeah. You?

                    JIM
          Yes. Well, I guess we can walk
          from here.

EXT. JIM'S CADILLAC. NIGHT.   161

Jim and Elena get out, shaky, from the car.

They pause for a moment.

The street lamp above them sizzles, but stays on.

They start to walk.

INT. LIBBETS' LIVING ROOM. NIGHT.   162

Paul and Libbets, still frozen in the same position. Finally,
Paul gently pushes Libbets' head back.

It slides off his leg and, as Paul lurches forward in a failed
attempt to grab it, Libbets flops backwards, her head hitting
the carpet with a dull but decidedly loud thump.

                    PAUL
          Oh, shit!

Paul gets up, looks down at her.

                              (CONTINUED)

CONTINUED:

She snores.

He runs over to a side table and sees the clock: 11:10.

> PAUL
> Oh shit oh shit.

He grabs his comic books and runs for the door.

INT. TAXI. NIGHT.   163

The driver impassively inches down Park Avenue.

> PAUL
> Oh shit oh shit.

INT. TRAIN. NIGHT.   164

Paul sprints into the train just as the doors are closing.

INT. TRAIN. NIGHT   165

Paul walks through the nearly empty train car and finds a seat.
He pulls his *Fantastic Four* comic book out of his coat pocket.

INT. HALFORD LIVING ROOM. NIGHT.   166

Ben makes his way into the living room and heads for the front
door. He pauses for a moment, smiles, and heads back for the
living room.

He goes to the bowl, and with a look of dawning self-
consciousness and a brief chuckle, pulls his keys out -- the
last set.

INT. SANDY'S ROOM. NIGHT.   167

Sandy and Wendy are sitting on the floor. He grabs his G.I.
Joe.

> SANDY
> Check this out. He's supposed to
> talk all kinds of stuff, but he's
> like malfunctioned.

He pulls the dog tag on the doll, and G.I. Joe emits a plastic
macho voice.

(CONTINUED)

CONTINUED:

                        G.I. JOE
            Mayday! Mayday! Get this message
            back to base!

                        SANDY
            Same thing. Again and again.

Wendy takes the doll and yanks the cord.

                        G.I. JOE
            Mayday! Mayday! Get this message
            back to base!

                        SANDY
            It's gonna get a lot colder
            tonight, I predict. Probably a
            blackout. Do you have candles in
            your house? I know where the
            candles are, and I have my own
            flashlight. Over there. Also, I
            know where every emergency exit is
            on this floor.

During the course of his monologue, as Wendy looks on, Sandy
calmly ties a noose for his doll.

                        SANDY
            This knot's called a bowline.

He puts the noose over the doll's head, as Wendy holds the doll
for him.

                        G.I. JOE
            Mayday! Mayday!

                        SANDY
            Let's hang him.

Sandy drapes the noose over the edge of a dresser drawer. G.I.
Joe dangles. They both look at him in silence.

The silence continues.

                        WENDY
            He's dead.

                        SANDY
            If it wasn't raining we could take
            him outside and blow him up.

                                        (CONTINUED)

                  WENDY
        He wouldn't blow up. He'd just
        get all mangled or twisted.

She takes the doll down and lays him flat on the bed. And then
begins to remove its clothes.

Sandy looks on, desirous.

                  WENDY
        Well.
            (noticing his lack of
             anatomy)
        It looks like someone got to his
        private parts before us.

                  SANDY
        Communist Viet Cong.

                  WENDY
        They left it in the jungle.

They speak with high seriousness.

Wendy slides up on the bed where Sandy sits, a pillow on his
lap, and one by one, with exaggerated slowness, she removes her
snowboots as if they were stiletto heels.

                  WENDY
        Can I get into your bed?
            (pause)
        With you?

Sandy begins to shake.

                  SANDY
        We -- we have to go to the guest
        room. We can't stay in here.
        What if Mikey? My parents?

                  WENDY
        Don't worry about them. They're
        at that party, getting drunk and
        falling all over each other and
        making jokes about McGovern and
        stuff.

Sandy begins to cry.

                  SANDY
        It's just -- it's just --

                 (CONTINUED)

CONTINUED: (3)   167

She takes his hand, and they walk out of the room and down the
hall, into the guest room.

INT. GUEST ROOM. NIGHT.   168

Wendy and Sandy enter. She sees the vodka bottle on the
dresser.

                    WENDY
          Want a drink?

                    SANDY
          Vodka?

                    WENDY
          You never tasted the stuff?

She fills the glass to the brim and hands the bottle to Sandy.

They clink and each toss back a sip.

Sandy coughs and gags, but swallows.

                    WENDY
          Try again.

He does.

                    SANDY
          It feels warm.

                    WENDY
          One more shot?

                    SANDY
          Okay.

They drink.

                    WENDY
          Under the covers.

Under they go, and soon every layer of clothing emerges.

                    WENDY
              (feeling her way)
          Get 'em off.

Sandy begins to laugh, and soon Wendy joins him.

They roll around on top of each other for a while.

                                        (CONTINUED)

CONTINUED:

                    WENDY
          Have you ever had a nocturnal
          emission?

                    SANDY
          Huh?

                    WENDY
          That's the name for when you wake
          up and find this little pool of
          sticky stuff, like after a sexy
          dream.

Sandy shakes his head.

                    WENDY
          They didn't tell you this stuff
          yet? What planet do you live on?

Sandy doesn't answer, but climbs back on top of her and kisses
her neck.

                    SANDY
          I love you.

                    WENDY
          That's nice. Are you drunk?

                    SANDY
          I don't know. How do I know?

                    WENDY
          I don't know either. You spin
          around, when you lie down.

Sandy rolls off her and lies on his back.

                    SANDY
          I don't think I'm spinning.

They cuddle up together.

He yawns. She yawns.

EXT. SILVER MEADOW. NIGHT.   169

Mikey walks along the edge of the empty pool in the rain. He
climbs up on the diving board and bounces lightly on it, but
then gets off and stands, looking down at the pool again.

EXT. SILVER MEADOW. NIGHT.   170

Mikey walks across the field. The rain is pretty much over.

EXT. STREET. NIGHT.   171

An odd stillness. The storm has let up, leaving icicles forming
on the tree branches and fence posts. Mikey walks along. With
a running start, he slides on the ice.

He walks back up and slides again, hollering with joy. He is an
image of a tiny yet absolute and positive freedom.

The streetlights sputter on, then off.

INT. CARVER GUEST ROOM. NIGHT.   172

Sandy and Wendy lie asleep.

EXT. STREET. NIGHT.   173

The same corner where previously Mikey, and later Wendy, paused.

A power line is down. It hisses and HUMS -- a humming very much
like the humming Mikey has been hearing earlier.

The humming takes on the same transcendent tonality to which
Mikey has become so accustomed at such moments.

Mikey sits down on a metal street guardrail, to ponder the sound
and the snaking coil of electricity.

A strange look of almost religious wonder overcomes his face, as
the power line connects to the guardrail.

                    MIKEY
          Oh, shit.

Glued by an electrical pulse to the rail, he shakes as the
current flows through him.

After a minute, his body slumps and slides down the road.

INT. TRAIN. NIGHT.   174

As Paul sits reading on the moving train, the lights inside
begin to sputter, and the train begins to slow.

                              (CONTINUED)

CONTINUED: 174

After a few moments, the train grinds to a halt, and Paul and
his few fellow late-night passengers are left in near total
dark, with only the light of an emergency exit sign above Paul's
head to light the scene.

The train is eerily silent.

EXT. HOOD CAR. NIGHT.   175

Ben drives home.

EXT. STREET IN FRONT OF CARVER HOUSE. PRE-DAWN.   176

Jim and Elena arrive on foot.

                    JIM
          You want to come in, get a cup of
          coffee -- warm up? I can either
          walk you home, or you could crash
          in the guest room.

                    ELENA
          Sure. Maybe coffee. Then a walk
          home.

She takes off her soaking wet shoes as she enters the house.

INT. CARVER KITCHEN. PRE-DAWN.   177

                    JIM
               (hanging up the phone)
          Phone's out. I hope the pipe's --
          ah --

He walks into the kitchen. The pipes have begun to burst.
There's a water leak running down the walls, forming a puddle on
the floor.

Elena has walked into the kitchen behind him. She leans against
the counter, picking up the garter belt without thinking for a
second, then putting it back down.

                    JIM
          Oh, well. Why don't you put on
          some dry socks -- and we've got
          some rain boots in the guest
          closet back there. Last room
          upstairs -- back of the hall.

                                                        (CONTINUED)

CONTINUED: 177

Elena climbs the stairs in her bare feet.

INT. CARVER GUEST ROOM. CONT'D.   178

Elena opens the door, and discovers Wendy and Sandy asleep. She
stands before the bed, and gazes down on them.

They look almost angelic.

Wendy, sensing her presence in the room, opens her eyes, slowly
coming out of sleep.

                    ELENA
               (heartbroken, softly)
          Get dressed.

Elena walks out of the room, back to the kitchen.

Wendy gets out of bed quietly, leaving Sandy sleeping
peacefully.

She looks at him lovingly, and tucks the blanket back up around
him.

INT. CARVER KITCHEN. PRE-DAWN.   179

Elena and Jim are drinking coffee.

                    ELENA
          You should let him sleep.

Wendy enters. She looks inquisitively at the two adults.

                    WENDY
          Where's Dad?

INT. HOOD CAR. PRE-DAWN.   180

Ben continues to drive slowly. He looks out his side window,
and sees something -- the glow of an orange parka. He puts on
his brakes.

EXT. STREET. PRE-DAWN.   181

Ben gets out of the car, and stands on the top of an icy
embankment. In a clump of bushes is Mikey's body.

                         (CONTINUED)

112.

CONTINUED: 181

He walks hesitantly toward it. Mike's body lies face down in
the wet slush.

Ben leans down and turns the body over, then stands back in
amazement and saddened shock.

He bends over the body, and tries a cursory, futile mouth-to-
mouth.

He stands back up for a moment, then picks Mike's body up,
carrying him over the hill and onto the street. We see now that
he is parked just a short block from the Carver's house.

He bypasses his car and walks directly down the street toward
the house. The effort is obviously enormous. He falls from
time to time, then gets back up.

INT. TRAIN. PRE-DAWN.   182

Various passengers asleep.

Paul, hunched up in his seat under the faint emergency exit
light, cold. He reads his comic book by the light of the
emergency exit.

                    "DON'T YOU SEE, SUE? HE WAS TOO
                    POWERFUL...IF HIS ENERGY HAD
                    CONTINUED TO BUILD, HE WOULD HAVE
                    DESTROYED THE WORLD!"

Suddenly, the lights begin to flicker on and the hum of the
train's engines returns.

The conductor enters the car, blasting forth in his classic
nasal train conductor voice.

                    CONDUCTOR
               Good morning ladies and
               gentlemen --

On Paul, squinting in the harsh light. We are back at the
flashforward from the beginning of the film.

EXT. TRAIN BRIDGE. PRE-DAWN.   183

The train moves slowly through a suburban, semi-forested
landscape. On the street below the bridge, an emergency highway
crew is removing a fallen tree, their trucks aglow in flashing
yellow lights.

INT. CARVER KITCHEN. DAWN.   184

Elena pours Wendy a cup of coffee. They're both in their coats.

                    WENDY
          I don't like coffee.

                    ELENA
          It'll warm you up.

Elena sits next to her. They both cross their legs, then raise
their cups and sip the coffee, not noticing the simultaneity of
their movements.

INT. GUEST ROOM. DAWN.   185

Jim watches the sleeping Sandy, picks up the half-empty bottle
of vodka, pours himself a drink. The noise wakes Sandy up. Jim
sits down on the bed at his feet.

                    SANDY
          Dad?

                    JIM
          Sandy.

Jim raises a quiet toast to his son and takes a gulp of vodka.

INT. KITCHEN. DAWN.   186

Elena and Wendy hear a hollering from outside, get up to see
what it is.

EXT. CARVER HOUSE. DAWN.   187

Elena and Wendy come out the front door, as Ben lays Mikey's
body onto the ground before the front steps.

                    ELENA
          Ben?

He's too breathless to speak.

They stand there, looking down at Mikey.

Behind Elena and Wendy, Jim appears.

He pushes softly by them toward the body of his son.

                              (CONTINUED)

> BEN
> Jim -- he was just up -- in
> Silver Lane -- I think maybe -- a
> power line --

Jim picks up his son.

He carries him silently into the house.

Sandy, now standing inside the foyer, pushes himself back
against the wall as they pass, without expression.

After a moment, from outside, the Hoods can hear Jim's wailing.

> BEN
> Do you think? Maybe we should
> call someone --

> ELENA
> The phone's out.

> BEN
> Yeah. Well, we can just --

> ELENA
> Ben, I don't know if he really
> wants us here.

Wendy has been watching Sandy through the screen door.

> WENDY
> Wait, I --

She turns back up the front steps and gently goes in --

INT. CARVER LIVING ROOM. CONT'D.   188

On the living room floor, Jim is hugging Mike's body, his
shoulders shaking uncontrollably, sobbing.

Wendy walks and stands next to Sandy, who is filled momentarily
with a brief inexplicable rush of anger toward her -- but she
takes him and gives him an awkward, childlike hug, then turns
and runs out the door, joining Ben and Elena on the driveway.
Sandy watches her go, his face wet with tears.

EXT. CARVER HOUSE. CONT'D.   189

                    ELENA
          Oh, you know, for a minute I
          thought it was --

                    BEN
          Paul? Yeah. You think --

                    WENDY
          He's probably been waiting all
          night at the station.

                    BEN
          C'mon.

EXT. STREET. DAWN.   190

Elena, Wendy, and Ben reach the car and get in. The car starts
and drives off.

There are now crews out cleaning up the storm's debris and
fixing the power lines as they drive.

INT. HOOD'S CAR. DAWN.   191

Wendy is in the back seat. As Ben drives, Elena looks over to
him. He catches her eye. They both turn their gazes back to
the road. But then, as if on cue, they look again at each
other.

Briefly, but deeply, they look and see each other.

EXT. CONRAIL STATION. EARLY MORNING.   192

The train slowly pulls in. The Hood family walks down to the
end of the platform.

The train doors open, and Paul, tired and a bit cramped,
emerges. He sees his family gathered at the other end of the
platform, and walks to them.

They stand, silent, even dignified, awaiting him.

When he joins them they all walk silently to the car and get in.

INT. HOOD CAR. EARLY MORNING.   193

Sunlight floods in and temporarily blinds Ben as he starts the
engine.

                                      (CONTINUED)

He squints, his eyes tearing a bit from the light.

He looks around, first at his wife, then at his two children sitting in the back seat.

He turns off the engine. Quietly, he begins to cry.

He turns to the back seat and smiles, crying, at his children.

>   ELENA
>   (softly)
>   Ben.

Paul looks at Wendy, silently asking her what's happening.

She casts her eyes downward, as does he.

>   ELENA
>   (her hand still not yet
>   touching him)
>   Ben.

EXT. STATION PARKING LOT. MORNING.   194

From above:

The car, the first morning light shining upon it.

STILLS

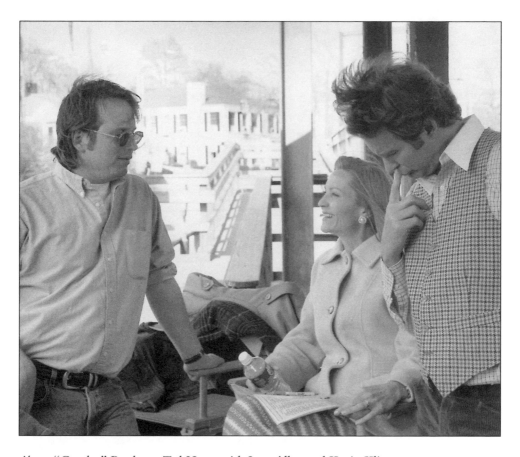

Above: "Gotcha." Producer Ted Hope with Joan Allen and Kevin Kline.

WENDY
Christina Ricci

JANEY
Sigourney Weaver

SANDY
Adam Hann-Byrd

PAUL
Tobey Maguire

BEN
Kevin Kline

ELENA
Joan Allen

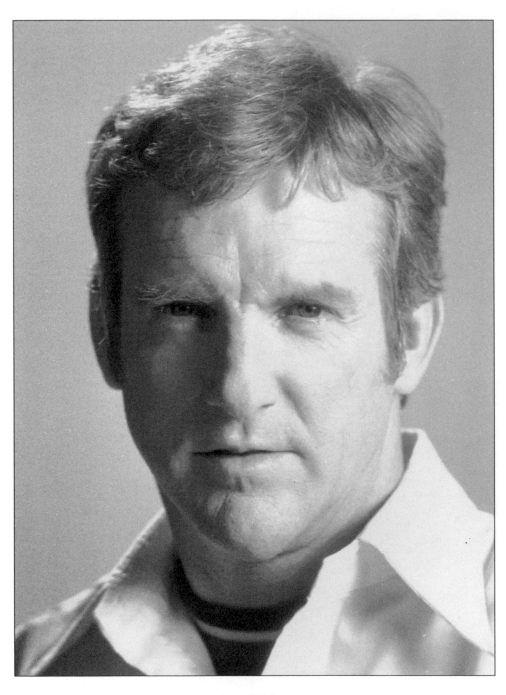

JIM
Jamey Sheridan

MIKEY
Elijah Wood

Above: "Into the void." Paul *(Tobey Maguire)* finds his family at the train station.

Below: "Anti-matter." Preparing the final scene at the New Canaan train station, the art department applies plastic icicles and the effects team's famous "splooge" under a sweltering sun: the thermometer hit eighty-five degrees during the shooting of the scene.

Above: "We actually enjoy it." Ben *(Kevin Kline)* offers the phone to Wendy *(Christina Ricci).*
Below: "Think of the money supply as a large male organ." Ben *(Kline)* philosophizes on
   the job.

Above: "Breaking down the old Unitarian barriers." The Reverend Edwards *(Michael Cumpsty)* talks shop with Elena *(Joan Allen)*.

Below: "You look very—free." Wendy *(Ricci)* testing the limits.

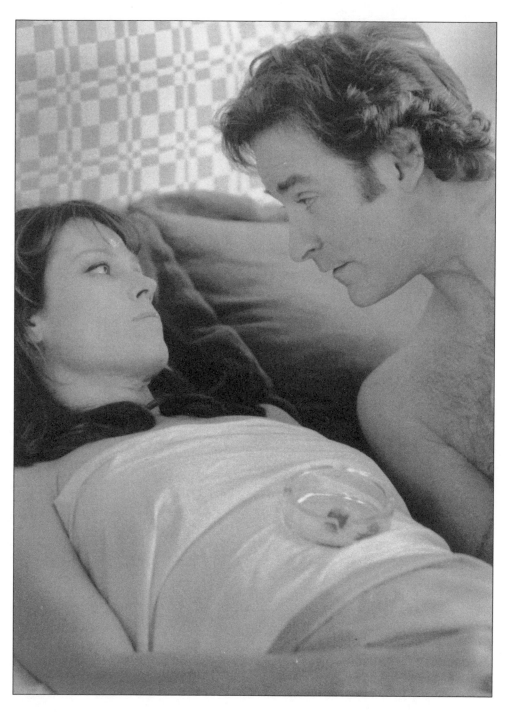

Above: "Your needs. My needs." Janey *(Sigourney Weaver)* and Ben *(Kline)* in the guest room.

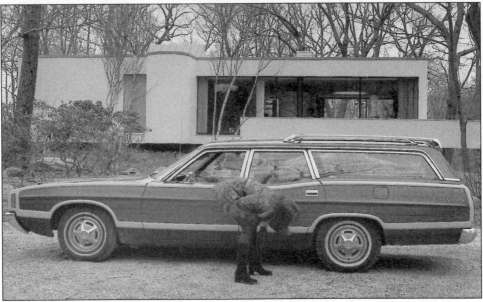

Above: "We've got to trade this thing in for a normal bed." Jim *(Jamey Sheridan)* returns home to Janey *(Weaver)*.
Below: "Going in all the way." Janey *(Weaver)* ducks for cover.

Above: "They were old. And they couldn't fly anyway." Sandy *(Adam Hann-Byrd)* at play.

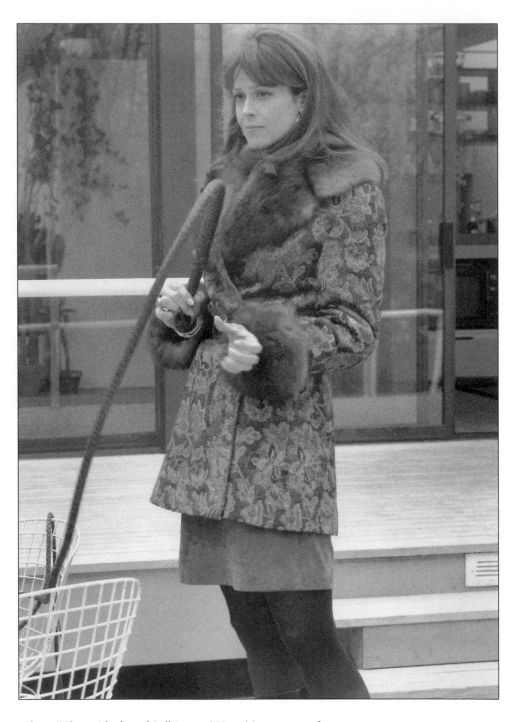

Above: "Play with the whip." Janey *(Weaver)* in a maternal moment.

Above: "I'll show you mine if you show me yours." Wendy *(Ricci)* initiates Sandy *(Hann-Byrd).*
Below: "In Samoa and in other developing nations." Janey *(Weaver)* lectures Wendy *(Ricci)* on
  the facts of life.

Above: "It's a one-on-one kind of date thing." Paul *(Maguire)* borrows Wendy's phone.
Below: "You used to love to say grace, remember?" Thanksgiving at the Hood house.

Above: "Even the invisible girl becomes visible." Ang Lee directs Joan Allen.
Below: "Birth control." Ben *(Kline)* does some imaginary golfing in his boxer shorts after Janey *(Weaver)* has ditched him.

Above: "I'll carry you." Wendy *(Ricci)* in her father's arms.
Below: "New this year." The key bowl is presented to a befuddled Ben and Elena *(Kline and Allen)*.

Above: "Strictly volunteer, of course." The keys.
Below: "A prior engagement overcame me." Janey *(Weaver)* clears the air with Ben *(Kline).*

Above: "Wait, this is the training, where they don't let you go to the bathroom?" Janey *(Weaver)* learns about EST from Neal *(Glenn Fitzpatrick).*

Above: "We're not going anywhere." Ang Lee rehearses the key party with a nervous cast as James Schamus looks on.
Below: "Another shot?" Sandy *(Hann-Byrd)* and Wendy *(Ricci)* prepare for bedtime.

Above: "It's special." Libbets *(Katie Holmes)* attempts to understand her aura.
Below: "Isn't it up to us?" The key selection begins.

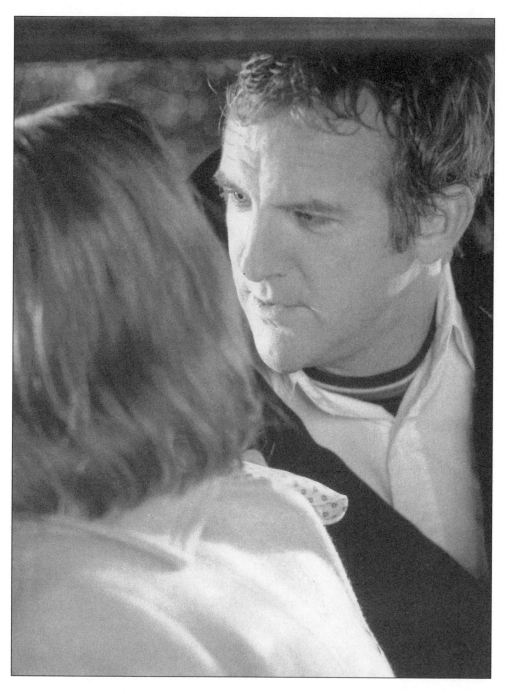

Above: "Do these seats go back?" Elena *(Allen)* and Jim *(Sheridan)* commence the briefest love scene in cinema history.

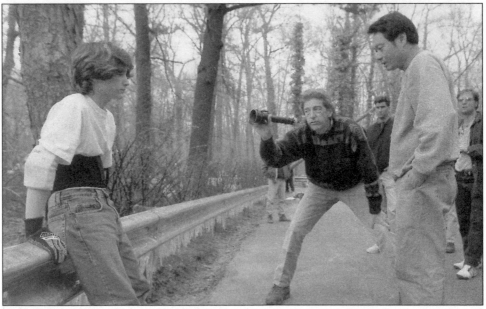

Above: "I don't think so." Elena *(Allen)* hands Jim *(Sheridan)* his car keys.
Below: "Oh, no." Cinematographer Fred Elmes and Ang Lee contemplate the final moments
of Mikey *(Elijah Wood)*.

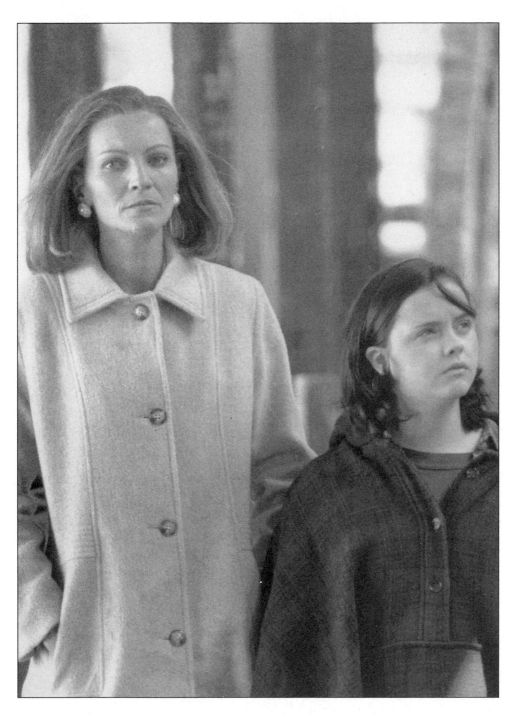

Above: "For a moment I thought it was…Paul." Waiting at the station.

SCENE NOTES

BY JAMES SCHAMUS

There are, of course, hundreds if not thousands of differences between screenplay and finished film. I will pass over in silence the vast majority of them and note only those that indicate the more important thematic and dramatic changes we made on the journey from script to screen.

Sc. 2-4: We simplified the voice-over as the combination of opening credits, comic-book images, text, music, and voice-over was simply too much information for anyone but Hal the computer to take in at the opening of a film.

Sc. 16: A mistake — Thai stick would have been purchased not by the bag, but by the stick.

Sc. 6-11: The entire therapy sequence was cut during production. This became part of a general movement away from the social satire and comedy in the script and toward a more focused dramatic structure.

Sc. 20-21: Much of the babble at the dinner party table was trimmed, mainly to pick up the pace of the sequence, as well as to ease up on the social satire.

Sc. 24: Omitted, mainly because we didn't have time to do an entire night exterior lighting setup solely for a few kisses good-bye.

Sc. 31-35: We decided to drop Janey and Ben's encounter on the train in order to give their affair a bit more of a history. It would have been a great comic scene for Sigourney and Kevin. . . . And the exquisite tragicomedy of Ben's "money supply as phallus" speech was also reluctantly cut during postproduction, along with his bantering with office rival George St. Clair, superbly performed by Henry Czerny, who can still be seen in the key party. Instead, well into the editing process, we realized that the early focus of the film had to remain rooted in New Canaan and in the more dramatic feelings of yearning and loss that were propelling the characters through the rest of the film. Ben's trip to work in New York was thus reconceived to be more of a melancholic interlude than a comedic sequence.

Sc. 36: The "humming" motif, which played prominently in the script as a kind of foreboding music of the spheres for which only Mikey's ears are available, was more or less removed by the final edit. Mikey's fate is fore-shadowed strongly enough through Elijah Wood's performance—we didn't feel the need to prop it up with sound effects.

Sc. 54: We removed this scene from the final cut of the film—a scene Ang cherished as one of the best acted and edited he'd ever directed—simply because Elena and Philip's interactions worked so economically in their other two scenes. This one was sacrificed for reasons of pacing and focus. Michael Cumpsty's depiction of Philip's essentially genial and lonely soul, Joan Allen's near caress of his hand at the end of the scene, and Kate Burton's hilarious take on the town gossip made this certainly one of the most painful cuts from the film—it was a near perfect scene. And Ang had gotten an entire background through the coffee shop windows depicting a long line of cars waiting for gas—a nice image that gave us both a taste of the 1973 oil crisis and an emblem of the crisis of consumption afflicting the community.

Sc. 59-64: Shooting a film that takes place during Thanksgiving in the spring had its pleasures as well as its terrors, and these scenes counted among the latter. We were able to shoot the interior car dialogue between Janey and Elena, as well as Elena being dropped off in town and her initial bike riding, but location scheduling and a host of other production issues left us shy of the pickup itself, just as virtually every tree, bush, and flower in New Canaan decided to bloom. We pushed the scene to the end of the production schedule, hoping to find an alternative treeless location, but by the final week of shooting realized we could live without the sequence as a whole— the brief interaction between the two women at the Carvers' dinner party told enough of the story.

Sc. 94: The masturbation speech, which in an earlier draft of the script actually served as the opening of the film, was much reduced in the editing—again, part of an overall strategy to decrease the comedic side of the film in favor of the more familial. Note the moody music that now plays under this scene.

Sc. 99-102: We decided not to shoot the pot-smoking in the bathroom scene and to drop the sports poster scene in the editing room, in order to craft the Thanksgiving day celebration as less of a sequence than as a kind of beat—a brief moment before the final descent of the last act.

Sc. 128-173: The entire final night was rearranged many times in the editing room, with each story line interwoven with the others a number of different ways until we ended up with a final solution to the puzzle. We always expected this to be so, because what can appear on the page to be decisive and witty crosscutting can seem labored and unfocused on the screen. Ang was also able to create a large number of thematic and visual echoes from scene to scene during the shooting, many of which worked in combinations we could hardly have surmised until after we commenced the editing process. In the end, Ben's pot smoking, Paul's call home to Wendy, Wendy's blasé attempt at "suicide"—all of these were cut while the rest of the scenes, especially the key selection sequence, ended up getting scrambled and reordered. Mikey's final words were changed from "Oh, shit" back to the book's original "Oh, no." Rick Moody rightly pointed out to us that the original emphasized Mikey's wonder while the script made him out to be too much the worldly teenager.

Sc. 187-188: During rehearsals Sigourney asked us about the fate of her character and talked about how she would see Janey at the end of the film. Ang immediately seized on her suggestions, and powerfully so. We had never wanted to bring Janey back to the scene in the living room. As a film scene, it would have called for a melodramatic response that would have been impossible to stage without pathos, and we were worried that it might look as though we were punishing her character for her independence and rebellion, something we very much wanted to avoid. But to see Janey's eyes flutter open as she awakes at the sound of her husband's cries and, from there, to imagine the rest of her journey seemed a far more just resolution to her story than simply omitting her from the final moments of the film, and Ang came particularly to relish, too, her return to the quiet house and her pause in front of the boys' room. As she curls up into a fetal position on the water bed, an object of comic derision earlier in the film, the movement and sound of the water serve as a subtle contrast to the hardening ice of the storm outside.

Sc. 194: As the editing of the film progressed, we began to understand that, however it could be accounted for, something of the novel's first-person voice was also emerging from the film—that, after all, it was Paul's story we were finally telling, even if we had constructed the screenplay as an ensemble work. We realized that it was appropriate to hear Paul's voice again in the moments after Mikey's death, both to recuperate somewhat from the shock of the killing as well as to fold the emotional registers of that shock into one primary consciousness. The voice-over we came up with for Paul is neither a summary nor a celebration; it avoids the direct reference to the comic book even as it builds from the worldview his reading of the book has developed during the previous voice-overs:

PAUL
(voice-over)

```
When you think about it, it's not easy to keep from
just wandering out of life. It's like someone is
always leaving the door open to the next world,
and if you aren't paying attention, you could just
walk through it. And then you've died. That's
why sometimes in your dreams it's like you're
standing in that doorway and the dying people
and the newborn people pass you by and brush up
against you as they come in and out of the world
during the night. You get spun around, and in
the morning, it takes a while to find your way back
into the world.
```

At the end of the film, it is Paul's face on which we finally hold. It is his vision of his father's tears through which he and, we hope, the film as a whole achieves a troubled but still liberating epiphany, a kind of embarrassment of forgiveness.

Ang and his production team spent months researching every aspect of American life in the seventies, and as preproduction progressed Ang began to pull from the research the essential themes and emotions he hoped to organize the film around. With the assistance of researcher Jean Castelli, he even put together a theme chart for the crew, which helped identify where he saw patterns and echoes that might inform each creative department's work.

Scene	Time/Day	Weather	Themes	Echoes	Motifs	Warmth
27. INT. WENDY'S ROOM (*Wendy on the phone*)	NIGHT				Nixon	
28. INT. HOOD UPSTAIRS HALLWAY (*Elena and Ben come home*)	NIGHT			look down hall towards kitchen with Ben/ Elena, like in Sc. 57		
29. INT. WENDY'S ROOM (*Ben says goodnight to his daugther.*)	NIGHT		inconsistent dad behavior		Nixon	parental affection: Ben and Wendy
29A EXT. HOOD HOUSE	NIGHT				establishing	
Day 4 Mon. Nov. 19						
30. EXT. NEW CANAAN TRAIN STATION (*Men in gray flannel suits off to work, c.1973*)	DAY WITH SUN				advertising images; train/commuting; power lines	
31. INT. TRAIN	DAY WITH SUN		pushing the limits (boredom)	Ben spaces out like Paul	advertising images; train/commuting/sex; power lines	
32. MANHATTAN OFFICE BUILDING	DAY WITH SUN			tunnel tilt to sky line, like Paul at night		
33. SHACKLEY AND SCHWIMMER CONF RM (*Stagflation*)	DAY WITH SUN		looking for patterns (macroeconomic)	displaced desire/frustration (cf. "facts of life")	'73 zeitgeist; distraction (Ben); glass + reflection	
34. INT. BEN HOOD'S OFFICE (*George vs. Ben at work*)	DAY WITH SUN		peer pressure: redefining/opening up institutions: up the organization	like father like son: Paul/Francis- Ben/George; Ben + Elena looking for meaning of life	'73 zeitgeist; aggression (George)	

CAST AND CREW CREDITS

Fox Searchlight Presents
A Good Machine Production
An Ang Lee Film

Kevin Kline

THE ICE STORM

Joan Allen	Tobey Maguire
Henry Czerny	Christina Ricci
Adam Hann-Byrd	Jamey Sheridan
David Krumholtz	Elijah Wood
and Sigourney Weaver	

Casting by
Avy Kaufman

Costume Designer
Carol Oditz

Associate Producers
Alysse Bezahler
Anthony Bregman

Composer
Mychael Danna

Based on the novel by
Rick Moody

Film Editor
Tim Squyres

Production Designer
Mark Friedberg

Director of Photography
Frederick Elmes, A.S.C.

Screenplay by
James Schamus

Produced by
Ted Hope
James Schamus
and Ang Lee

Directed by
Ang Lee

CAST

listed in alphabetical order

elena hood . . . . Joan ALLEN
dorothy franklin . . . . Kate BURTON
ted shackley . . . . William CAIN
philip edwards . . . . Michael CUMPSTY
george clair . . . . Henry CZERNY
mrs. gadd . . . . Maia DANZIGER
pharmacist . . . . Michael EGERMAN
marie earle . . . . Christine FARRELL
neil conrad . . . . Glenn FITZGERALD
train conductor . . . . Tom FLAGG
ted franklin . . . . Jonathan FREEMAN
weather reporter . . . . Barbara GARRICK
stephen earle . . . . Dennis GAZOMIROS
sandy carver . . . . Adam HANN-BYRD
mark boland . . . . John Benjamin HICKEY
libbets casey . . . . Katie HOLMES
dot halford . . . . Allison JANNEY
pierce sawyer . . . . Byron JENNINGS
sari steele . . . . Colette KILROY
ben hood . . . . Kevin KLINE
jack moellering . . . . Ivan KRONENFELD

francis davenport . . . . . . David KRUMHOLTZ
weatherman . . . . Daniel McDONALD
paul hood . . . . Tobey MAGUIRE
mr. gadd . . . . Miles MAREK
maria conrad . . . . Donna MITCHELL
helen wentworth . . . . Barbara NEAL
claudia white . . . . Nancy OPEL
dave gorman . . . . Larry PINE
wendy hood . . . . Christina RICCI
mikey's teacher . . . . Marcell ROSENBLATT
pharmacy attendant . . . . Wendy SCOTT
jim carver . . . . Jamey SHERIDAN
woman in pharmacy . . . . Evelyn SOLANN
marge . . . . Jessica STONE
beth . . . . Sarah THOMPSON
janey carver . . . . Sigourney WEAVER
paul's teacher . . . . Scott WENTWORTH
rob halford . . . . Rob WESTENBERG
mikey carver . . . . Elijah WOOD

stunt coordinators . . . . G.A. Aguilar
Douglas Crosby

stunts . . . . Jill Brown
Danny Downey
Lizzie Olesker
Susan Trout

unit production manager . . . . Alysse Bezahler
1st assistant directors . . . . Stephen Wertimer
James W. Murray, Jr.

2nd assistant directors . . . . Lisa Rowe
Brian O'Kelley

post production supervisors . . . Anthony Bregman
Kelly Miller

supervising sound editor . . . . Philip Stockton

re-recording mixer . . . . Reilly Steele
SOUND ONE

1st assistant editor . . . . Susan Littenberg

production supervisor . . . . Nancy Kriegel

2nd 2nd assistant director . . . . Linda Perkins

art director . . . . Bob Shaw
assistant art directors . . . . James Feng
Paul Kelly
Nicholas Lundy

art department coordinator . . . . Paige Bailey
set decorator . . . . Stephanie Carroll
assistant set decorator . . . . Jennifer Alex
storyboards . . . . Brick Mason
researcher . . . . Jean-Christophe Castelli

leadman . . . . Peter Dunbar
key set dresser . . . . Kelly Canfield

product placement & clearances . . . Wendy Cohen
asst. to production designer . . . . Tina Khayat
art department assistants . . . . Alisa Grifo
Robin Thomas
Mary Wigmore

set dressers . . . . Billy Bishop
Debbie Canfield
Scott Canfield
Charlie Foster
John Harajovic
Etienne Martine
Michael Murphy

Patrick Murphy
Peter Nauyokas
Mario Presterone
Paul Richards
Barret Schumacher
Paul Wilson
Kelly Winn

on-set dressers . . . . Jim Lillis
Travis Wright
charge scenic . . . . Elizabeth Linn

scenic forepersons . . . . Katy Dilkes
James Hoff

camera scenic . . . . Robert Barnett
key scenic shop person . . . . Emily Gaunt
scenic shop persons . . . . Tom Noucias
Chris Ruzek
shop production assistants . . . . Rob Landoll
Jesse Peliken

scenic artists . . . . Eric Bart
Steve Barth
Steve Caldwell
Marshall Carbee
Lauren Doner
Judy Evans
Michael Greene
Christopher Hébel
Richard Jones
Eugene Kagansky
Arcady Kotler
E. Reynold Maher
Vietta Maher
Michael Miles
Don Nance
John Paul
Cheryl Stewart

construction coordinator . . . . . Thomas Costabile
construction foreman . . . . Mark Mann
key carpenter . . . . Christopher J. Noonan

carpenters . . . . Judson Bell
Jack Coyle
Robert Dillon
John Farrell
Ed Gangloff
Claude Horstman
John McHugh
Genarro Proscia
Thomas White

key construction grip . . . . Robert W. Schmitt	electricians . . . . Michael Gallart
construction grip best boy . . . . Billy Van	Jamie Gallagher
construction grips . . . . James Brown	Timothy Healy
Joe Casillo	additional electricians . . . . Joseph R. Bruck
John Farina	Peter C. Caldwell
Ashalon Jones	Andy Niceberg
Monique Mitchell	Paul Steinberg
Vincent Reilly	day generator operator . . . . Daniel Canton
Frank Vigilante	
	rigging gaffers . . . . John Cardoni
camera operators . . . . Phil Oetiker	Peter Walts
John Sosenko	best boy rigging electric . . . . . Donald W. Schreck
	rigging electrics . . . . Bob Blair
1st assistant camera . . . . Andy Harris	Kobkeo Phothivongsa
2nd assistant camera . . . . Adam Gilmore	Perry Wolberger
camera loader . . . . Patrick Quinn	Chris Zizzo
video assist . . . . Ed Gleason	
24 frame playback . . . . Dennis Green	shop electrics . . . . David Levine
	Myron Odegaard
2nd unit photography . . . . Frank Prinzi	Brandon Odegaard
steadicam operators . . . . Andy Casey	key grip . . . . Jimmy Finnerty
Rick Rafael	best boy grip . . . . Tom Kerwick
	dolly grip . . . . Brad Goss
still photographers . . . . Adger Cowans	company grips . . . . Tony Campenni
Barry Wetcher	Joe Donahue
	Bill Jones
sound mixer . . . . Drew Kunin	Dave La Rue
	Bill Weberg
boom person . . . . Mark Goodermote	additional grip . . . . Steven E. Lawler
utility person . . . . Jeanne Gilliland	
	key rigging grip . . . . Jim McMillan, Jr.
property master . . . . Mark Peltzer	rigging grips . . . . Jim McMillan, Sr.
assistant property master . . . . Wally Adee	Tim McMillan
additional props . . . . Jonathan Tessler	
picture car production asst. . . . . Jacquie Hurd	make-up artists . . . . Michal Bigger
	James Sarzotti
stage manager . . . . Eric Zoback	assistant make-up . . . . Katie Bihr
assistant stage manager . . . . Virginia Plath	Frances Kohler
	ms. weaver's make-up . . . . Linda DeVetta
lead greensperson . . . . Will Scheck	
greens foreperson . . . . Graydon Pihlaja	hair stylist . . . . Aaron F. Quarles
greenspersons . . . . Pedro Barquin	assistant hair . . . . Donna Spahn
Guido DeCurtis	
Sean Lynch	associate costume designer . . . . Elizabeth Shelton
Darius Menard	wardrobe supervisors . . . Melissa Adzima-Stanton
Dominick Toto	Tom Stokes
standby greensperson . . . John "Butch" McCarthy	asst. to costume designer . . . . Leslie Yarmo
	wardrobe production asst. . . . . Anastasia Leopold
script supervisor . . . . Mary Cybulski	seamstress . . . . Laurie J. Buehler
gaffer . . . . Jonathan Lumley	wardrobe intern . . . . Frank Alberino
best boy electric . . . . Gary Hildebrand	location supervisor . . . . Declan Baldwin for
	FEATURELINE INC.

assistant location managers . . . . David Martin
                                        Mike S. Ryan
location coordinator . . . . Shannon Bowen
location scouts . . . . David Graham
                                        Greg McHale
location production assts. . . . . Laura Franses
                                        Janet Henry
                                        Ashley Sieg

production coordinator . . . . Beth A. Boyd
asst. production coordinator . . . . Libby Richman
production secretary . . . . Ryan Allen
office production assistants . . . . Chris Elam
                                        Dean Haspiel
                                        Stuart Nicolai
                                        Matt Whitcher
production intern . . . . Bryan O'Cain
nyc office liaison . . . . Deidre Schrowang

asst. production manager . . . . John Rath
assistant unit manager . . . . Melissa Marr
set production assistants . . . . Jennifer M. Blais
                                        John Craig
                                        Apoovra Lakhia
                                        Deanna Leslie
                                        Alison Russo
                                        Gregory John Smith
set intern . . . . Tracy Moore
film runner . . . . Paul Fischer

special effects supervisor . . . . John Ottesen

special effects . . . . Edward Drohan III
                                        Edward Drohan IV
                                        George Drohan
                                        Greg Hagler
                                        Daniel Ottesen
                                        Ronald R. Ottesen, Jr.
                                        Rich Pashayan
                                        John Rapp
                                        Ted Suchecki

assistant to mr. hope . . . . Hetakaisa Paarte
assistants to mr. lee . . . . Susanna Horng
                                        David Lee
assistants to mr. schamus . . . . Sig Libowitz
                                        Santiago Navila
                                        Jessica Weigmann

auditor . . . . Craig Cannold
assistant auditor . . . . Olimpia T. Rinaldi
payroll accountant . . . Theresa Giardino Finnerty
accounting assistant . . . . Christine Hoppe
casting associate . . . . Julie Lichter
extras casting . . . . Judie Fixler
extras casting coordinator . . . . . Alyson Silverberg

unit publicists . . . . Jeff Hill, Millys Lee
                                        CLEIN + WHITE

transportation captain . . . . Jimmy Nugent

drivers . . . . Bob Anderson
    Frank Appedu   Paul Kane
    Ed Blacknick   Joe Mallon
    John Brady   Bobby Martini
    Ted Brown, Jr.   George Moran
    Jack Buckman   Robert Morgan
    Jim Cablusky   Regis J. Mullaney
    Steve Chartrand   Kevin O'Neil
    Matt Calley   Danny Poseidento
    Mike Canosa   Bob Rohr
    James H. Chlebowski   Frank Scarvy
    Tom Colovito   Kevin Smith
    Richard Euell   Mike Stowe
    Bobby Featherstone   Ray Sullivan
    Al Gardner   Dan Thelen
    Dan Haughton   John Uberti
    Tony Ingrassellino   James Williams
    Lenny Luizzi   Frank Young

parking coordinator . . . . Jose Tejada

tutors . . . . Rhona Gordon
                                        Karin Nystrom
                                ON LOCATION TUTORS

craft service . . . . Gillian Malone
                                        Martina Pozzi
caterers . . . . COAST TO COAST CATERING
                        MAINE COURSE CATERING

2nd assistant editors . . . . Ian Silverstein
                                        Yasmine Amitai

sound effects designer . . . . Eugene Gearty
dialogue editor . . . . Fred Rosenberg
ADR Editor . . . . Marissa Littlefield

foley supervisor . . . . Bruce Pross
foley artist . . . . Marko Costanzo
foley editors . . . . Frank Kern
                                        Kam Chan
assistant sound editors . . . . Julie Lindner
                                        Chris Fielder
                                        Benjamin Cheah
                                        Todd Milner
                                        Glenfield Payne

apprentice sound editor . . . . Gasuza Lwanga
sound effects intern . . . . Alan Zaleski

post production sound . . . . C5 INC.
sound coordinator . . . . Ghretta Hynd

ADR recordists . . David Boulton SOUND ONE
Andy Kris SPIN CYCLE POST, INC.

music editor . . . . Pat Mullins
asst. to music supervisor . . . . . . Maisie Weissman

projectionist . . . . Edmund Nardone

titles by . . . . BUREAU, N.Y.

digital visual effects by . . . . BALSMEYER &
EVERETT, INC.
supervisor . . . . Randy Balsmeyer
producer . . . . Kathy Kelehan
compositing supervisor . . . . Daniel Leung

train miniatures by . . SESSUMS ENGINEERING
Jack Sessums
Gary Maxwell
Michael Sajbel

post production accountant . . . . Joyce Hsieh
post production assistants . . . . Glen Basner
Ross Katz

negative cutters . . . . Stan & Patricia Sztaba
technicolor color timer . . . . Gloria Kaiser

dolby stereo consultant . . . . Tim J.Carroll

gamelan music by the EVERGREEN CLUB
GAMELAN ENSEMBLE
Bill Brennan
Mark Duggan
Paul Houle
Blair MacKay

north american native flutes . . . Daniel Cecil Hill
conductor . . . . Christopher Dedrick
orchestration . . . . Jamie Hopkings

score recorded and mixed by
Brad Haehnel at MANTA EASTERN SOUND,
Toronto

DIRTY LOVE
Written by Frank Zappa
Used by Permission of Munchkin Music
Performed by Frank Zappa
Courtesy of Rykodisc

SAMBA TRISTE
Written by Baden Powell & Billy Blanco
Used by Permission of Fermata do Brasil Ltda.
Performed by Stan Getz & Charlie Byrd
Courtesy of Verve Records
By Arrangement with
PolyGram Film & TV Licensing

TWO-PART INVENTION
IN B-FLAT MAJOR
Written by Johann Sebastian Bach
Performed by Wendy Carlos
Courtesy of Sony Classical
By Arrangement with Sony Music Licensing

SUAVECITO
Written by Richard Bean,
Abel Zarate & Pablo Tellez
Used by Permission of Canterbury Music
Performed by Malo
Courtesy of Warner Bros. Records Inc.
By Arrangement with Warner Special Products

SUGAR SUGAR
Written by Andy Kim & Jeff Barry
Used by Permission of EMI
Blackwood Music Inc. (BMI)
Performed by Wilson Pickett
Courtesy of Atlantic Recording Corp.
By Arrangement with Warner Special Products

THE MORNING AFTER
Written by Al Kasha & Joel Hirschhorn
Published by WB Music Corp. (ASCAP)/
Warner-Tamerlane Publishing Corp. (BMI)

I GOT A NAME
Written by Norman Gimbel & Charles Fox
Published by Warner-Tamerlane
Publishing Corp. (BMI)
Performed by Jim Croce
Courtesy of Saja Music Co.

TOO LATE TO TURN BACK NOW
Written by Eddie Cornelius
Used by Permission of EMI
Unart Catalog Inc. (BMI)
Performed by Cornelius Brothers & Sister Rose
Courtesy of EMI Records
Under License from EMI-Capitol
Music Special Markets

MONTEGO BAY
Written by Jeff Barry & Bobby Bloom
Used by Permission of EMI
Unart Catalog Inc. (BMI)
Performed by Bobby Bloom
Courtesy of Polydor Records
By Arrangement with
PolyGram Film & TV Licensing

O GRANDE AMOR
Written by Antonio Carlos Jobin
& Vinicius De Moraes
Used by Permission of Ipanema Music Corp.
Performed by Antonio Carlos Jobim
Courtesy of Verve Records
By Arrangement with
PolyGram Film & TV Licensing

COCONUT
Written by Harry Nilsson
Used by Permission of EMI
Blackwood Music Inc. (BMI)
Performed by Harry Nilsson
Courtesy of the RCA Records
Label of BMG Entertainment

LIGHT UP OR LEAVE ME ALONE
Written by Jim Capaldi
Used by Permission of Island Music Ltd.
Performed by Traffic
Courtesy of Island Records Limited
By Arrangement with
PolyGram Film & TV Licensing

HELP ME MAKE IT THROUGH THE NIGHT
Written by Kris Kristofferson
Used by Permission of Combine Music Corp.
Administered by EMI Blackwood Music Inc. (BMI)
Performed by Sammi Smith
Courtesy of Dominion Entertainment, Inc.

MR. BIG
Written by Andy Fraser, Simon Kirke,
Paul Kossof & Paul Rogers
Used by Permission of Blue Mountain Music, Ltd.
Performed by Free
Courtesy of A&M Records, Inc./
Island Records Limited
By Arrangement with
PolyGram Film & TV Licensing

COMPARED TO WHAT
Written by Gene McDaniels
Used by Permission of Lonport Music Corp.
Performed by Les McCann & Eddie Harris
Courtesy of Atlantic Recording Corp.
By Arrangement with Warner Special Products

LEVON
Written by Elton John & Bernie Taupin
Used by Permission of Dick James Music Ltd.
Performed by Elton John
Courtesy of Mercury Records Limited
By Arrangement with
PolyGram Film & TV Licensing

NIGHT LIGHTS
Written by Gerry Mulligan
Used by Permission of
Mulligan Publishing Co., Inc.
Performed by Gerry Mulligan
Courtesy of Verve Records
By Arrangement with
PolyGram Film & TV Licensing

I CAN'T READ
Written by David Bowie & Reeves Gabrels
Used by Permission of
Jones Music America (ASCAP)
Administered by RZO Music
Performed by David Bowie
Courtesy of Jones Music

Soundtrack from The Track Factory

President Nixon's News
Conference at San Clemente,
August 22, 1973. Courtesy of the
NIXON PRESIDENTIAL MATERIALS Staff
and the NATIONAL ARCHIVES

Divorce Court Courtesy of
RHODES PRODUCTIONS, Jack Rhodes, Sr.

Green Hornet Courtesy of
George W. Trendle, Jr., and
TWENTIETH CENTURY FOX TELEVISION

Ruffles Courtesy of
DAVIE-BROWN ENTERTAINMENT
on behalf of FRITO-LAY INC.

Vanishing Minds Courtesy of
THE COLLEGE FUND,
UNITED NEGRO COLLEGE FUND

M★A★S★H Courtesy of
TWENTIETH CENTURY FOX TELEVISION

Room 222 Courtesy of
TWENTIETH CENTURY FOX TELEVISION

Keep America Beautiful Courtesy of KEEP
AMERICA BEAUTIFUL, INC.

Time Tunnel Courtesy of
TWENTIETH CENTURY FOX TELEVISION

Special Thanks
NEW YORK CITY MAYOR'S OFFICE OF FILM,
THEATER AND BROADCASTING
Towns of Greenwich and New Canaan, Connecticut
Gayle Carpenter, Superintendent Robert Pegues,
Administrative Officer Peter G. Murphy: TOWN OF
NEW CANAAN, CONNECTICUT
Lieutenant Stephen Seiter (OIC&C),
Lieutenant Eric Weiner: STATE OF NEW YORK,
DIVISION OF MILITARY AND NAVAL AFFAIRS
Dante Brown, Claude Cargill, Cecil K. Watkins:
HARLEM TENNIS CENTER and THE HARLEM
JUNIOR TENNIS PROGRAM,
NANCY KRICORIAN LITERARY GROUPING

Art Contributions
Fritzi Ahadi, Rico Fonseca, GEMINI-G.E.L.,
Los Angeles,CA, Ellsworth Kelly, KRAUSHAAR
GALLERIES, INC., Mon Levinson,
Roy Lichtenstein, Peter Max, Leroy Neiman,
Robert Rauschenberg, Jodi Scherer
CASTELLI GRAPHICS, VAGA - VISUAL
ARTISTS, Sherle Wagner

UPSTAIRS / DOWNTOWN ANTIQUES
GRACIOUS HOME

Selected Jewelry provided by Johnny Lu
Ms. Weaver's Jewelry provided by Stephen Dweck

CONVERSE, CPC INTERNATIONAL,
DRAKES CAKES, CULINAR, ELLIOTS
AMAZING BEVERAGES, HAMMERMILL PAPER,
KASHI CEREALS, KIEHLS SINCE 1851, M&M
MARS CO., NEUTROGENA,
PENDLETON WOOLEN MILLS, PEZ

payroll . . . . ENTERTAINMENT PARTNERS
insurance . . . . Ross Miller,
Amy Schultz DISC INSURANCE
projector equipment provided by . . BOSTON LIGHT
AND SOUND
opticals by . . . . THE EFFECTS HOUSE
post production editing services by . . . . GOOD EDIT,
INC
lenses and Arri ® cameras by . . . CAMERA SERVICE
CENTER
dailies by . . . . DUART FILM & VIDEO
color by . . . . TECHNICOLOR
prints by . . . . DELUXE

ABOUT THE AUTHORS

ANG LEE was born in Taiwan in 1954 and moved to the U.S. in 1978 where he received his BFA in theater from the University of Illinois, and his MFA in film production from New York University. In 1983 he won the Taiwanese Golden Harvest Film Festival Best Narrative Film award for his film *Dim Lake*. While at NYU he made *Fine Line,* which received Best Director and Best Film at the 1985 NYU Film Festival.

Pushing Hands, Ang Lee's first feature screened in the Panorama section of the 1992 Berlin Film Festival, won Best Film in the Asian-Pacific Festival, was nominated for nine Golden Horse awards (the Taiwanese Academy Award) and won three, including a Special Jury Prize for Ang Lee's direction.

In 1994, *The Wedding Banquet* premiered at the Berlin Film Festival (1993) and was awarded Berlin's top prize, The Golden Bear. The film garnered tremendous critical praise and box office success. *Variety* heralded it as "the most profitable film in the world in 1993." The film was nominated for the Academy and Golden Globe Awards for Best Foreign Language Film and six Independent Spirit awards. In Taiwan, *The Wedding Banquet* received five Golden Horse awards, including awards for Best Film and Best Director.

Eat Drink Man Woman, the third film in Ang Lee's "Father Knows Best" trilogy, premiered as the opening night film in the Director's Fortnight at the Cannes Film Festival (1994) and was nominated for Academy and Golden Globe Awards. In addition, the film was voted Best Foreign Language Film by the National Board of Review.

In 1995, Ang Lee directed *Sense and Sensibility,* starring Emma Thompson, Hugh Grant, and Kate Winslet, with a screenplay by Thompson. The film was nominated for seven Academy Awards, including Best Picture, and won the Oscar for Best Screenplay Adaptation. In addition, the film received the Golden Bear Award at the Berlin Film Festival, as well as Golden Globes for Best Screenplay and Best Film. One of the most critically acclaimed films of the year, *Sense and Sensibility* was featured in over 100 Ten Best Films lists for 1995, and was lauded by the New York Film Critics (Best Director), the Boston Film Critics (Best Film, Best Director), and the National Board of Review (Best Film, Best Director).

In 1996, Ang Lee completed *The Ice Storm,* his first feature on an entirely American subject, which was adapted from the acclaimed novel by Rick Moody, and stars Kevin Kline, Sigourney Weaver, and Joan Allen.

JAMES SCHAMUS founded the film production company Good Machine with Ted Hope in 1991, the year he also began teaching in the film division of Columbia University's School of the Arts. In the six years since Good Machine's founding, Schamus and Hope have emerged as two of the most critically and commercially successful producers in the independent film world. Among Schamus's credits are the films that have resulted from his longstanding collaboration with the director Ang Lee: *Pushing Hands* (1991, Producer and Co-Writer); *The Wedding Banquet* (1992, Producer and Co-Writer); *Eat Drink Man Woman* (1993, Associate Producer and Co-Writer); *Sense and Sensibility* (1995, Co-Producer); and the forthcoming *The Ice Storm,* starring Kevin Kline and Sigourney Weaver (Producer and Writer). Among the other twenty films with which Schamus has been associated are four of the past six Sundance Film Festival Grand Prize winners: Edward Burns's *The Brothers McMullen* (1995, Executive Producer); Tom Noonan's *What Happened Was...* (1994, Executive Producer); Alexandre Rockwell's *In the Soup* (1992, Associate Producer); and Todd Haynes's *Poison* (1991, Executive Producer). Schamus also served as executive producer on Haynes's *Safe* (1995). At Columbia University, Schamus teaches a wide variety of courses, from the history of the film musical to an introduction to film theory. This screenplay for *The Ice Storm* was awarded Best Screenplay Prize at Cannes.